The Forest is the Path

GARY LIGHTBODY

The Forest is the Path

HarperCollins*Publishers*

HarperCollins*Publishers*
1 London Bridge Street
London SE1 9GF

www.harpercollins.co.uk

HarperCollins*Publishers*
Macken House, 39/40 Mayor Street Upper
Dublin 1, D01 C9W8, Ireland

4wordhouse and Polydor Label Group are divisions of
Universal Music Operations Limited
4 Pancras Square
London N1C 4AG
fourwordhouse.com
www.polydor.co.uk

First published by HarperCollinsPublishers and 4wordhouse,
on behalf of Polydor Label Group, 2025

1 3 5 7 9 10 8 6 4 2

© Gary Lightbody 2025

Gary Lightbody asserts the moral right to
be identified as the author of this work

A catalogue record of this book is
available from the British Library

Lyrics from 'Everything's Here and Nothing's Lost', 'Waking Up Now' and 'These Lies', by Snow Patrol,
courtesy of Universal Music Publishing Group (UMPG)

While every effort has been made to trace the owners of copyright material reproduced herein and
secure permissions, the publishers would like to apologise for any omissions and will be pleased to
incorporate missing acknowledgements in any future edition of this book.

Main edition ISBN 978-0-00-875190-6
Special edition ISBN 978-0-00-877230-7

Printed and bound in the UK using 100%
renewable electricity at CPI Group (UK) Ltd

'Between what is said and not meant, and what is meant and not said, most of love is lost'
Kahlil Gibran

'Mostly it is loss that teaches us about the worth of things'
Arthur Schopenhauer

Contents

Introduction

Hi. What follows is really a companion piece to the latest Snow Patrol album of the same name, and while you don't have to read this book to understand the album, a listen to the album might help some parts of this book make sense. There are references to the album in here at times and song lyrics are dotted around within it. Not that I'm giving anyone homework to do. In the words of Fleetwood Mac you can, of course, go your own way. It is though, the album I am most proud of in our thirty-year career.

Half of the book explores a few of the main themes of the album – time, love, etc. The other half is spent in the time before we made this album. This half of the book tells the story of my dad, Jack's, death and the numb journey it sent me on. The end of this journey seemed to unlock the part of me that had been immobilised and dormant and I started to write songs again, which would become the first songs written for this record. Not to give away the ending or anything, but just so you know this book is not one of wallowing. There is a purpose to it. I mean, I hope.

At one point in the book I mention the Oasis lyric 'don't put your life in the hands of a rock 'n' roll band'. Sound advice indeed. None of what follows is me trying to tell anyone how to live their life or how to deal with death or grief. Heaven forbid. This is simply what happened to me and how I met it with varying degrees of success and failure. If it helps anyone in their own grief I would be thrilled to be of service in any small way, but I would never have the temerity to expect it. Really, it's simply me trying my best to live without bumping my head or falling down too much.

I also don't want to tell anyone definitively what the album and book title means in case it's different to what you'd imagined, but perhaps one way to think of what 'the forest is the path' means is that maybe, just maybe, it's the things that happen off the beaten track in our lives that end up being the most significant. The things we didn't, or couldn't, plan for. Jean de La Fontaine said that a person 'often meets their destiny on the road they took to avoid it'. It's hard to prepare for the things that we cannot imagine. Like the death of a parent.

To all the people, friends, family, SP fans, that have been kind enough, over the years, to say to me that I should write a book, and have encouraged me to do so – and I waved off the compliment thinking I just could never be able to sit still long enough to write one, even a short one – thank you all. It seems I just about sat still long enough to write one.

A short one.

JACK

Part One

December 2019

You're falling through time so all I can do is fall with you.

The numbness had set in long before I sat at your bedside. But even with senses impaired as the flight touches down at Belfast City, I can somehow still feel the screeching of wheels on tarmac scorching something deep into me. The wound freezes inside me though, the second it's born, and it will take me a full year to locate it, never mind to begin to heal it. Driving to the nursing home for your last days I watch houses I have seen thousands of times whip past like strangers, or are they now old friends who no longer want to know me?

Inside my mind 'Don't Go' by Hothouse Flowers wafts about softly. Aimlessly. Seeming to emanate, barely a whisper really, from some far-flung ramshackle church left to ruin in an untended, grown-wild corner of my mind: 'Don't go, don't leave me now, now, now. While the sun smiles, stick around laugh awhile, yeah.' The muffled echoes of the song begin to blossom into a gentle nudging of insistence, like the scratching of a dog awake at your door begging you awake too, and you know you can do nothing but comply, because it knows no other way to be, and it will not stop until you let it in. Don't leave me now, now, now. I'm awake damn it, but, please, don't make me open the door to this.

But if we're all honest, you left us a long time ago. Dementia took you and I'd like you back please so I can say goodbye to my father. I know he's in there. But it doesn't work like that. You're gone and going, and here's me driving towards you, too numb to feel the wound slashed fierce across my heart, and far too numb to ever really know what your ending even felt like.

I arrive passing nursing staff that give me the look. The look that says death is soon. They all loved you, bless them. That has always been clear every time I have visited here. You were a cantankerous so-and-so at times, but a charmer right enough. And funny as hell. The nurses say everything without saying a word. We've had some false alarms over the years with you but when I got to whatever hospital or nursing home those alarms were ringing in, there were none of these looks. Those looks were of relief. These looks are new, and they signal the start of the end.

I'm in the room now and there's mum and my sister, Sarah, but who in god's name is this on the bed? An apparition in the vague shape of my father, nought but a skeleton, a wisp, draped in something pallid that could be skin. If it is skin I swear you could almost see through it. But I think it is you. I just don't want it to be.

Your breathing is a laboured cacophony eerily matching the plane wheels scorching the runway in me. The two noises take turns pummelling me, like tag-team wrestlers. Every breath looks and sounds like you are trying to suck life into you from great distance. And maybe a million miles from here, the curling tail-end of each breath just barely catches a single atom of life and hauls it roaring back into you, helping you to cling on for another moment. But there are clearly not that many more moments left. These are the last ones. And, after all that time I could have asked you any number of things and never bothered my arse, now rushing towards me are all the myriad questions I have for you, and they line up on a bench in my mind like skydivers waiting to be pushed, riding in a battered old plane that will never get high enough for a safe jump. So I will never know, never ever know, anything more about you, from you. Only what others will say in the following days, weeks, months about you. But not what you would say to any of this. I can only guess. So my questions just sit there. Ghosts in their first moments in an eternal purgatory. The brutality of the realisation cuts so keenly I touch my face to see if there's blood.

A few days from now my mum will hand me your wedding ring and ask if I would like to have it, and for want of something to say, I say ... OK. I will hold that wedding ring in my hand and say to it, 'I am so sorry for letting you down so many times, I am sorry for being a terrible son. I am so sorry dad.' But I won't cry. I won't cry for a full year. Because of that I will assume many times that I am broken, and that I am awful. And instead an emptiness will take up residence in me and the numbness of the lack of you will devour everything I see and feel. My synapses will be severed and I won't know how to reattach them. I'll never know. One day they do eventually reattach and just start working again somehow, but I won't really know how, or why. The shame I will feel from all this though, will hang from me for the rest of my life. But I'm getting ahead of myself.

Each of your universe trawling breaths seem to suck in the walls of the room with it. The little room concertinas and shakes.

I don't say any of this out loud, or share it with anyone today, or for a long, long time. I decided there and then that my job is to hold this. This sharp, jagged object whose spikes are so copious that removing one from your skin is only possible by letting another pierce it, like the maw of some great beast. But I know I have to hold it all the same. And to shut up for once. To be the dutiful son for once. To be *here* for once. I was, am, always away somewhere, on tour or wherever, and now I need to be here. For whatever comes. Perhaps subconsciously I forced myself not to cry that day and my punishment was not to be able to cry for a whole year. Some curse drawn like blood from the pages of an Irish fairy tale. It's poetic maybe. Poetic justice perhaps for being absent for so much of what had passed these last years of your cognitive decline and illness.

To see you now, like this, and also know the man you were – a titan, a giant whose shadow I used to hide in – is hard to bear.

The nurse I hadn't noticed come in is leaving the room; the door closes behind her with a muffled crunch that in my head sounds like a distant gunshot and I'm falling backwards through my memory to the marshy edge of Strangford Lough in the dark, pulling ache of an almost new day.

I have slipped through years. Decades.

Is *your* life flashing before *my* eyes? Is that even a thing?

Strangford Lough is still as death. No rain, for once. No wind either. The sun announces its arrival with an almost imperceptible tonal shift. The dawn seems to come to the surface of the water first, as if the lough is draining the light from the sky before there is enough to light them both. Either that or the world is on upside down. The scant slow slivers of waves harness that stolen sky light and are kissed on top with little flecks of gold. As the black sky lightens to dark blue, I start to see where we are for the first time. We had trudged out here in the deepest part of the night through soupy mud that comes close, a few times, to spilling into my wee wellies. I'm only five years old. Maybe six. Even if I wasn't quite six yet I'd certainly be telling anyone that asked that I was 'nearly six'. Not five, god no. They'd be under no illusion as to my almost six-ness. But out here it's just me and my colossal father squelching our way through what feels like endless marsh to get to some mythical spot he likes to shoot at things from. Things like ducks. Things I don't want to be shot, but I keep schtum coz all I want at this age of nearly six is to spend time with my dad. And he wants to shoot things. So here we are stomping out in the almost daytime to shoot some things. My hand enveloped in his. Lucky, as he has to literally pull me up and out of the hungry mud each time it doesn't want to let me go. I look up at him towering above me and he turns his head to speak. BEEP, he says to me. I'm confused. BEEP, again. I don't understand.

BEEP! Louder this time and I'm back here beside you while you haul in another dreadful breath.

We are a constellation within a constellation. The sum of all the actions and events of our life compounded exponentially with the sum of the actions of every ancestor that passed the torch on, and on, and on, through millennia until we ourselves are custodians of that flame for the briefest of flickers in time. Your shift with the light is all but done now, so I'm left holding it, looking around for someone to pass it to. There is no one. No progeny of my own. So do I let this torch just fizzle out in my hand?

At your bedside we play some songs we think you liked. Hard to know for sure if you liked much of any music. The only song we know you loved for certain was Judy Garland singing 'Somewhere Over the Rainbow'. The incongruity of your toughness set against that song's sad sweetness always tickled me. And not to mention one of the only times in my life I recall seeing my father cry was when he was listening to it. It will be the song we play at your wake as the mourners leave the funeral home. It will be the thing that breaks most of the gathered.

The room is swallowing again, chewing me in its mouth like gum. I close my eyes to make it stop but instead slide away, along the blade of time, which cuts me in half and lands the pieces in our garden in the early 80s. You and I are kicking a football back and forth and my sister is on the swing you poured into concrete a few years back that will be rusted out in a few years hence – and will remain so in most of my memories of our old garden. Finding this swing of ours in a fairly decent condition takes me by surprise. If my memory can be wrong about this detail, can it therefore be wrong about everything? Yes. The answer is yes. None of this is real. And all of this is real. It happened exactly like this. It never happened at all. It is happening now. It is always happening. The ball gets away from me and rolls behind the gooseberry bush that we never made jam from. The garden sings with sunshine and the faint drift of 'Somewhere Over the Rainbow' hangs like the future over the summer evening. There is happiness everywhere. Bees bumble and wasps, erm, wasp from bush to flower and the fresh cut grass trimmings kick up with the spin of the ball as it is passed between us like a conversation.

There is a slant to our garden that always felt tiring. It made the ball speed away in one direction and struggle in the other. And in the struggle the weather turns suddenly. A great shadow falls on us. The gradient of the garden starts to increase. The ball rolls away and off the end of the world. The swing with my sister still seated on it hangs down in suspension, parallel to the now vertical garden, and she holds on for dear life. I slide away, my father too. I cling to an apple tree you planted whose apples we never ate, and you cling to the other side of the same tree. We're alright, son. We'll be OK. But your grip comes undone and I reach my eight-year-old hand out to grab hold of you but I'm not strong enough to keep you. The bottom of the garden is now a raging waterfall of all the things we ever had, and the house, the car, the dogs, and everything else stored in my memory of us then, tumbles away over and into the waterfall and you follow with it, with me watching your face as it's taken by the water. I hang from the apple tree, my six-year-old sister crying out for her father on the swing that never actually rusts, and was never rusted and will always remain pristine because my memory cannot be trusted. The apple tree and the swing you planted for your daughter and your son hold on. And they both hold on too. As quickly as it appeared the waterfall vanishes and the garden is flipped back as it was, and everything I watched fall is restored, and I hit the ground beside the tree and my sister is catapulted off the swing as it pendulums back with some gusto and lands her up the garden a fair bit. Everything lost is back in its right place, everything returned that was taken by the waterfall and the chaos. Everything except you.

Your bed takes a laboured breath of its own. The noise drags me out of whatever the hell that was by the hair. It, your bed, is a strange contraption alright. Inflating and deflating with each intake and outtake, making a grinding and crumpling sound that seems to be trying to sing an angry, tuneless duet with your dislocated breathing.

And, here beside you, sitting in your last embers, as I phase in and out of context, this is how I discover for myself that time does not run in a straight line. Rather we are encased in time. Past, present, future all happening at once if we can only slow down enough to see it, to feel it. Einstein once said, 'The only reason for time is so that everything doesn't happen at once.' But everything is happening at once. Time is unchained from its links. In the coming days, months, years I'll find you alive on too many occasions to pay much attention to the rules of time anymore. I'll see you, and I'll hear your voice everywhere I go.

To be here at the end of a life of a person that one thinks of as immortal is the slowest one can be. You can see and hear your own birth, and death, and everything in between. You can hear blades of grass growing, aching like new teeth. You can feel the continents swim apart from each other. You can feel the earth spinning on its axis. And you can see the end of everything and know that just past there is the start of everything else.

The world has smashed me to pieces so I can be rebuilt, but one has to want to be. I resist this for too long and there are pieces missing when I am eventually reformed. I have to fashion those parts from other things I find along the way: branches from the forest; salt from the sea; and from all the love I ever pushed away because I was afraid to be loved.

The sensation we sometimes get when we are sure that something happened yesterday but it actually happened 20 years ago is because it was both. To me it becomes the only truth of the universe. It did happen 20 years ago, and it did happen yesterday. That day you left us was the first day I felt this. It's the first day I understood that I truly know nothing. That I am emptied and refilled by history, and future, and today, and never. You are here still as I type these words now. But I also watched you go. I can still feel your warm hand in mine and also feel your concrete cold forehead in that same hand. Both now, both then, both forever. Both never.

Years from now I will know what to say to you in this moment and I will say it. I will know how to feel in this moment and I will feel it. I will tell myself when I get there and it will seem like the future but it won't be. It will be today.

*   *   *

You're gone now. Dead about an hour. The extended family arrive in your room. We stand around you like a fire that just went out wondering how the hell we keep warm now. There are tears. None from me though. It may look to those congregated like stoicism or bravery but it is neither. It's simply that the mechanism is broken. Crying is not available but if you hold the line one of our operators will be with you shortly, your call is important to us. I feel a hand inside my brain trying to press the button that would usually trigger tears but it just clicks on and off without function. We'll need to get a guy in to have a look at that, says a voice I don't recognise from deep within me. So I stand here doing nothing but occupy space, taking shallow sips from all that air you left behind.

The strangest thing is that in the days and hours right before you died, I knew you had fallen below speech. Post-lingual. I knew the only sound you'd make until the end was the raking howl of your breath. But, strange I know, now you've actually died I keep expecting you to say something. To puncture this way-too-quiet room filled only with the family's faint crying and the contrasting thunderous silence of everyone trying to think (without success) what the hell to say to my mum, my sister and me. But aren't we supposed to get some last words from you? Famous last words in fact. Where the fuck are those?! All your dad catchphrases leap around in my head like hyperactive rabbits daring you to wise up, stop faking it and join in: 'You're like a bull in a bloody china shop, Gary,' 'Ack, c'mere til I put my toe on you, ya ballix' and (on numerous occasions in my childhood while looking at a freshly grazed knee I got from falling hard on driveway gravel) 'Oh, that's a bad one, it'll have to come off at the neck.' These are just some of your many greatest hits, ready and waiting for you to sing them. Once more for the cheap seats eh, Jack? No? Come on old man, it'll take more than death to shut you up, surely? But nothing from you. I'm beginning to think this is serious.

The tears of others have started to grate on me a bit now. Not because they aren't warranted or from a deep place of love, they are, but because I don't have any to add to the pile. Always was one for joining in with the crowd, a world-class people pleaser, me. But now the crowd has gotten too far ahead of me and I'm wheezing, hunched over, hands on knees a few streets back.

I hear Colonel Brandon's voice calling from Jane Austen's pen, 'Give me an occupation ... or I shall run mad,' so I look for a task. Any task. Someone needs to go with the doctor to get the death certificate and run it up to Bangor town hall. These quaint arcanities and mundanities of death are, what I am imagining, just the salve I need. Or at the very least they are reassuringly neutral and probably won't involve anyone crying near me. So me and my old pal Davy, who has arrived to pay his respects, bless him, follow the doctor in her car. It starts the clock on one of the stranger hours of my life.

The doc sets off in her car like some fella just waved a chequered flag and Davy and I try hard to keep up. She actually – and I'm not kidding, this really happened – even runs a red light at one point. We're stuck at that red, firstly waving at her frantically trying to get her attention, then eventually descending into uncontrollable laughter at the ridiculousness of being beaten in a race we didn't sign up for on a day when everything else felt so goddamn slow. The laughter, while welcome in its way, seems far too loud to me. Everything seems too loud. The traffic and the outside world. And the silence. Christ, the silence is so loud I think it will destroy me.

We arrive at the clinic and I find the doctor, not without some difficulty given the labyrinthine halls of the place. When located I say, 'Did you just run a red light?' 'No,' she says, and gives me a look that suggests I should lay off the crack pipe. My brain can't take this. Did I just imagine it all? I resign myself in that moment to her side of the story and bookmark my immediate surrender in the situation for something I can beat myself up about at a later date. But right now I figure it's better to be in someone else's dream than my own. It's only later I get shoved back into my own when I ask Davy, 'Did I imagine her running a red light?' 'No mate, you didn't … You definitely did not.'

The doc hands me the death certificate. *Heart failure* I see written on it, as if that explains anything. Surely, we all die of heart failure. But I then realise I'm now holding a piece of paper in my hands that proves my dad is dead. A *certificate* of his death in fact. I start to remember the certificates of my life. Swimming 10 metres, cycling proficiency, grade one on the recorder. Jesus, it's a big leap from those to DEATH! Swimming, cycling, recorder, death. And there are pieces of paper to prove them all. It's real now. Still no tears but there seems something new in me. A river that once flowed so freely, but that I had never even noticed, has now turned to ice. The warm flowing waters of my blood invisible to me until now freeze and crack through my chest like livid blue lightning. So I can now see into my own chest? OK. X-ray vision, my new useless superpower. Shame I haven't even a lick of medical knowledge to do anything about what I find in there. So it's the least helpful superpower of them all. Well, I once had a dream that my superpower was that my hand could get really big. So big that at one point of expansion it would topple onto its fingertips and my body would hoist up and hang behind it like a scorpion tail. So this is more helpful than *that*. But barely.

So, I have a certificate of your death, and we are on our way to the town hall. Bangor, my home town, where I was born and a place I love dearly and deeply, is now a city but we still say town to each other. We may cough and laugh and correct ourselves, oh sorry I meant city, but our eyes betray us and say town in spite of us. All the same, I guess when I die someone will have to take a letter much like this one to the *city* hall. Today though, we're driving towards the town hall. This time at a normal pace as we are no longer hot on the tail of a rally-driving doctor.

The town hall is shorn of all humility and calls itself Bangor Castle. The name suggests a great towering, expansive citadel replete with arrow turrets, a drawbridge, a moat, perhaps cauldronfuls of boiling oil to be heaved over onto invading armies? But if you're looking for all those, you'll be disappointed. This particular castle is more like a big house. A nice big house right enough. But a castle? No. In I go to the castle and there are two women with kind eyes behind the reception that give me an 'ah it's yourself' look and I gurgle something about a death certificate, looking lost, but they seem to understand me enough and it unlocks the next level of this grim game without too much extra enquiry. 'Follow me,' the notary says and so I do. I'm malleable enough now to follow anyone just about anywhere. If she led me out onto the street into oncoming traffic I would waddle faithfully behind her like the tallest duckling there ever was. She doesn't though. Lead me into traffic I mean. And I'm grateful to her for that. Instead I'm led to a wee room that seems to fill in at the same speed as the death-info she punches into the computer. Honestly, I don't think there were four walls to this room when I walked in, but there's four when I walk out. It's as if the animator of my life that should have been drawing the parameters and interiors of my day fell asleep on the job, then woke up with a start, and had to hurriedly draw the walls of this room in while I wasn't fully paying attention. And while I'm fazed out still, the notary asks me questions which some other part of me answers. The auto-pilot has full control. The captain of me being asleep it seems, same as the animator. Is everyone fucking asleep in there?! Date of birth, address, name, cause of something, something else, etc., ... all answered by not me. He sounds like me, but not me. I think she's done now with the form and could be talking about the band. Ward Park maybe. Yes, I say every now and again and hope the yeses are in the right places.

Something of the wee, hastily completed office puts me in mind of school. Perhaps it's the dark walnut of the book shelves or the deep scratches on the weathered desk that pushes me even further away from the muffled words of the notary. All the way to my 4th-form English class. Our new English Literature teacher Mr McKee is about to read some poetry. I have yet to properly pay attention in school so I don't have any idea that what is about to happen is going to change my life forever. It will be the bell that rings me awake. The lightning that lands perilously near you but not on you: so a message, not a curse, from the gods. Mr McKee clears his throat, himself unaware, but perhaps hopeful, that he is going to change someone's life in these next moments.

'Between my finger and my thumb
The squat pen rests; snug as a gun.'

Heaney's words spill out of him in a thick Coleraine accent that is, to this day, the true tone of this colossal, earth-shaking poem to me. I can hear it in my head still in that same voice. Some artefact that was woven into my blood for safe keeping. It whistles through me sometimes like a nor'easter.

As the words come one after another, like the deceptively simple first steps of every epic journey, I feel it happening. I swear to god I felt it in that moment. I can't explain it fully but it was like a new music I had hungered for somewhere too deep to be felt on the surface, in need of itself to unlock itself. It was the map, the door and the key combined. By the time of the poem's refrain and the last four words – 'I'll dig with it' – I was upright. Keen. Fizzing.

What the fuck *was* that?! Mr Lightbody? Eh? What? Oh? Sorry? Yes, thank you. Back in the castle and we're standing up now to leave the recently drawn room. My father reduced to data on a screen. Deceased. I notice on the computer as I leave the room, a fresh page open for the next few dead, the cursor blinking lonely on the screen, line-blank-line-blank-line-blank. I know how it feels. It is exactly like me in this moment, just waiting for someone to punch the details in.

We walk out, myself and the notary, through the narrow halls and for something to say, I guess, she offers, 'Well this'll be something I can tell my kids about later.' It takes me a few days to hear it properly as, in that moment, my autopilot is still stuck on. I think as it happened, I tried to make her feel OK for saying it. I know there was no harm meant, she only wanted to fill the palling silence. But those words will echo in me a long time. In them my numbness and my family's pain are already demoted to dinner chit-chat around strangers' tables.

In the car again and back to the nursing home to find my father still dead from before. It is becoming clearer and clearer to me that this might be a chronic condition. When we arrived in the car park, we bumped into a guy that plays guitar each week for the folks in the home and he tells us my dad, every week without fail, requests 'Chasing Cars'. This is just about the sweetest thing my dad has ever done but he's gone and got himself far too dead for me to talk to him about it. Something else to add to the list of things unsaid. The guitarist smiles and enquires how is the old fella anyway? The truth won't solidify enough inside me yet to make a sound, so I hear myself saying 'ack he's fine'. And there's an easiness to the lie I don't enjoy but I shake off, for the moment at least.

We are told someone from the funeral home will come and collect the body. The body?!

The body. Just the meat? Just, the gammon? With death cracked over it like an egg. I look at what's left and try to find him in it. As I said before, I had the strongest feeling in those first few seconds after the last breath fell from him that he might say something. That he'd sit bolt upright, tell a few jokes, throw a wildly inappropriate comment at us and with *big finish* energy proclaim 'had yous all going'. But that was before the seal of the room was broken. I left, and so I let the air out of everything. Off I went to do those two strange tasks and must have dragged something unseen out with me, or perhaps while letting the door swing closed behind me, I snapped off the last scant thread we had to him, or him to us. But whatever's changed in the fabric of all this I know I'm to blame for it. And that feeling of hopefulness that he may have had a few last words, has been replaced with a terrible stillness. The doldrums, sailors call it. That remote slice of equatorial ocean vacuumed clean of air, wind and life itself. A purgatory you must have alternative means of propulsion to escape from because the natural elements have betrayed you and your sails ain't catching wind. So we'll need an engine to pull-rip the world to life again, and no one thought to bring one, so everything has stopped. The inertia though, has an uneasy paradoxical pull to it all of its own. Like when you're standing on the edge of a cliff and there is nothing pushing you, nothing near you, nothing tugging on you, and yet you can't help but feel a drag on your bones, on your soul, on your thoughts . . . jump. Just fucking jump. My mind snaps back to realise I'm leaning further over his bed than I thought I was and in doing so I puncture the frostbitten atmosphere that has congealed and domed around him. Even without touching him I know he's cold. It thrums off him like the heat of a great furnace. He burns with cold. And this is where I find him again. It seems to animate him just enough for me to feel him. He's cold. That means he's something. He's not nothing. OK, I can work with that.

In a different vehicle now, my sister's car, and we find the streets outside just as we left them. Not sure how everything can be so resolutely the same as it always was, but it is. Bangor is just as Bangor as it was before he died, and I may have to bend to its will, coz it likely won't bend to mine. All the same I begin to paint a great forest over everything I see. Plants and trees spring up everywhere, verdant and incorrigible. Houses begin to green and bark over, transforming into great oaks and pines and foliage. And as their windows smash with the force of trunks and solid yearning branches driving through them, the glass shatters to water, first like rain, then streams, now rivers. The trees line those rivers' banks and they surge ever upwards and expand ever outwards until they kill the sun to everything but their own canopy. All else below glowers and huffs in the darkness. The eagles that circle above will see only green below them as if there has always only been green, and always will be. An island of emerald. I read somewhere that in the Ireland before us, an epoch ago, the trees were so multitudinous that a squirrel could hop, branch to branch, from Derry to Cork. This is the land I see now. But not as the eagle. I am instead underneath, slated for digestion in the deep belly of it. Tangled and choked within roots and the unforgiving darkness of millennia. There is no way out, no way through. Any and all would-be paths close the second I see them, taunting me like torches fizzling out in a sprawling midnight maze. And now I too am turning to bark, to leaves, to soil, until I become just another fragment of the forest. My breath is caught now, caught by the mycorrhizal. It is, I am, only beats and bleeps in the neural networks of the forest floor. I come back online in the car with a heave, as if shoved out onto a stage I was refusing to perform on. I look around to see if anyone noticed. It would seem not. My mum and sister clearly thinking their own thoughts of death, Bangor, forests, eagles, or anything and everything except those things.

Our butts are parked in half-comfortable chairs in a waiting room in the funeral home. We were shown in by a nice lady who was sorry for our loss. He's not lost I think to myself, sure we were looking at him the whole time. But of course I make the noises I have heard from others in the reverse. 'Ah bless you. You're very kind.' In our chairs the three of us kindle laughter from things he said a while back. He was a very funny man so it is easy to find these little vignettes and hang out in them so we don't have to hang out in here. We've another form to fill in. Glory be. So many are the forms of death. You may cease but the bureaucracy cannot be stopped. It's like the terminator. But with clipboards. It all just keeps going. Is there comfort in that? I look around for some, find none. Dates and times are scribbled in but not without some small light-hearted disagreements. 'Was that the rosemary park house? Did he say he wanted to be . . .? Was it when yer man there with the thing? No it was the other fella.' We gradually untangle his life, stretch it out before us on the three separate living-room floors of our minds and find neat little places for it all on the form.

I mention my mum and sister at times and perhaps you may wonder why I don't go into more detail about them; it is because what they went through looking after dad in his last years was not what I went through. Their story is not mine to tell. They are the kindest, strongest, most thoughtful, big-hearted people I know and I love them more than I can put into words, and am beyond grateful to them for all they did for dad, but their stories belong to them alone. And whether they shared my numbness in that moment I don't know as we didn't talk about it but none of the three of us had any tears to offer. I think we were all just in shock.

When you began to leave us, you left us little clues.

'He's forgetting things. Did you hear me I said he's forgetting things?' 'Ack he's fine.' 'But you're not here, you wouldn't know.' That conversation with my sister lunges up to me from the well of time and rips out my windpipe. I rub my neck and feel the shame that lives in the sting of it. I didn't believe her then. Or should I say I didn't want to. Of course, I would eventually. And here we are now organising the salient details of your life into columns and it's all just so damn convenient I want to fucking scream. Shouldn't it be messier than this? Shouldn't we have to fill these forms in during a hurricane, or while being chased by a swarm of bees, or at the very least while being poked by a curious panda bear with a stick of bamboo. OK, so now I just want the last one to happen because it would be cute, but I'm serious about all this being worryingly simple. They've made it all so effortless since we arrived. I don't know what I expected and whether I imagined having to complete various tasks like some second-rate Indiana Jones trying to steal an Incan artefact from an ancient temple. But all this ease is becoming uneasy to me.

We are then led off to the room of coffins. They don't call it that, that would be off-putting, but that's what it is. It's a room full of coffins. Oh and there are also some urns. And now we have to pick one. Picking a coffin for one of your parents to be shoved into has to be the very bottom of the list of all the things you'd like to be asked to pick in your lifetime. I'd rather be standing in front of a stable of race horses and be asked to pick which one I would like to be kicked in the testicles by. But here we are, choosing a coffin like we're picking out a new couch. The woman from the funeral parlour, as kind and helpful as she is, is also describing the virtues of various death boxes and I try hard to listen to her as best as I can while also trying to detach myself from what this is really. We pick one, lost in my memory, it was made of some kind of wood, I know that. It comes to me then, the reason why all this ease is making me feel so disquieted. It is because you would've argued with us on all of this. We'd have filled the forms in wrong. We'd have picked the wrong coffin. Hell, we'd have even driven over here using the wrong route. I laugh to myself, inside of course, when I realise it. As easy and smooth as this is going, you wouldn't have signed off on any of it. My laughter dismantles though when I realise the actual truth of why I feel uncomfortable in the ease of it all. I don't want it to be easy on me. I want it to hurt. I want to be punished by it all. I want the universe to demand from me all the time I wasn't there for my family and I want it to take it from me, from my flesh and bones and future. I want to be punched in the face by every fucking moment that I didn't want to admit you were sick. You used to say 'I want I want never gets.' 'OK then dad, *please may* I be punched in the face by every fucking moment?'

Later that night I don't know how to sit down, and so I wander around my house unsure of what to do next. Without breaking stride on the way past it I pick up a photo I took of mum and dad about a year ago. They are sitting across from each other laughing. Everything is OK in there so I climb in and stand across from them and listen to the light-hearted banter and laughter of a good day. I shake it like a snow globe and let all the better pieces of us float around and then settle at our feet. I'm happy to find there are an awful lot of them. I'll stay in here for a little while and count them. Come find me when you figure out what the hell happens next.

ALBUM THEME 1

Time

April 2022

'Time isn't like an arrow
It's more like an axe that falls on you
And past can be future
Happening in present day'

From 'Waking Up Now'

I'm awake, just. In the dream I was flying as if an eagle over a vast forest canopy. Below me the myriad greens of the countless treetops roll like waves and when I lift my head to scan further it seems endless, infinite. The speed of me digs the wind into my feathers but I do not feel cold or hot or much of anything past the quickening of velocity and air in combination. Suddenly I turn downwards, towards the verdancy, and let the forest hurl itself up at me, falling now not flying, no longer an eagle, just a man. I've heard people say you go unconscious long before you hit the ground. Either that or you wake up. Johnny and I are in a rented house in Somerset at the start of the third day of writing what would become this album. All of us, Johnny, Nathan, Fraser T. Smith and myself, would have musical ideas that would spark songs to life for this record, but most would materialise during these sessions with Johnny and me, and this was the first of those. This was the only away trip as the rest of our writing sessions would happen at J's place in London but it all started here, in unfamiliar territory, for a reason. To get out and away from what might be familiar, or comfortable.

Time passes faster in the mountains than it does at sea level, so Carlo Rovelli told me. Not personally, rather from the pages of his book *The Order of Time*. As I try to make sense of it, in turn it begins to make some sense of me. My head in the future, my feet in the past. There is no time, Rovelli says, that we would recognise anyway, in the quantum world. The more powerful the lens of the microscope, it seems, the further we look down into what we are made of, the less time makes any sense at all. Maybe this is why I've felt, in the years since my dad passed, that time is not flowing forwards anymore. Not consistently anyway. It seems to stagger and bend and warp and dilate. Reading his book I ponder it is perhaps because I have been looking too closely at the smallness of everything. Focusing perhaps on the pieces of us that never die, our atoms and everything below them, in some bid to conjure immortality. If one looks down low enough to the ground of oneself, I mean really squint up close with your readers on and look only at all those lovely atoms of yours, you will never die. You will never ever die. So here's me on all fours squinting at myself and everything I love and have loved, trying to find all the parts of it, all that has been scattered to the four winds. So if I can perhaps gather them all up, pile them up and keep them safe, find and collect every single atom of every single person I love, or have ever loved, then they will never die. I will have beaten time. Time won't roll on if I just refuse to let it. I'm stubborn like that.

We wanted to start this album, as much as possible, from scratch. A blank page. The usual way we write songs is one of us would plink something out on the guitar or piano and I would come up with a vocal melody and sing gibberish words over it. Then I would, at some later date, take that melody away to a hidey-hole on my own and write lyrics into it. Johnny suggested that this time, instead of that I should try and write the words there and then, here and now, in the room, in the moment. It was a new way of writing lyrics for me and I was intimidated by the concept at first. However, on the very first day we wrote 'The Beginning' and I wrote every word of it that day too. So the little experiment worked. For a day anyway. But, then the second day came and went and we had written 'Everything's Here and Nothing's Lost', and, same thing, I wrote the lyrics for it that day too. So here we are on the third day about to start something else. I have a wee idea on my phone voice notes from a wee while back. Just the makings of a chorus, scratched out on a guitar, with the words 'you never really tire of it' sung over it. Not much to go on really but J extracted the chords from my creaky guitar scratchings and reformed them on the piano, pouring steel and weight into them, and immediately it sounded like we might be onto something. He then worked his magic adding a few more instruments, the man can play everything, so I set about writing some words.

Johnny and Nathan have no idea I am harvesting their atoms, neither of them realising I am following after them vacuuming their sluffed-off remainders and filing them away. I'll build all this again and we'll live all this once more. Time will repeat because I will make it repeat. I will be there this time for the ones I love. I'll not be gone. I will never let anyone down again. But I know that is not true because I already have. If you look hard enough you can see the comet tail of all the debris trailing behind each of us, all that is leaving. But what you don't see if you only look at what is lost, is what remains and what is rebuilt. Our cells renew every seven years. We are reborn. New people, top to bottom. Anyone that says people don't change isn't looking closely enough. I am too caught up in what we are leaving behind. 'Get present', I hear in meditation and yoga classes. 'Be in the now.' If you know, can you please tell me where now is and I'll try to get there, be there. Point to it, point to it on the map.

The previous two days as I said I had managed to get the words done each day but I had allowed myself to edit and change whatever I wanted to. I mean, a song is alive, it can and will and should be allowed to change shape as many times as it needs to make sense. Today I want to try something else. Just let whatever falls from the pen fall. No edits, no changes, just a stream of consciousness. Johnny was building the track and it was already beginning to sound mighty. I let myself be lost. No mind. Is this the now? If this is now it is some other now. So then, by definition, this is not now.

Everything falls away like a continental shelf. I saw a video once of a free diver swimming down to the edge of that shelf and then beyond into what was all just a vast darkness. I have some sense of my arm being connected to my shoulder and all that 'knees and toes, knees and toes' bullshit, and I know the pen is in my hand because I left it there before I started swimming down here, and I feel the pushing of ink onto paper but more like when I had surgery on my ear and I was awake and they just numbed the ear and all I felt was tugging. I feel the ink being tugged out by the page.

When I come to, I see the words that found their way into my Moleskine book, but I don't remember. After I finished it, I imagined I would cheat sometime in the future (I mean who would know, it's not like I'm gonna write a book about all this) and I would rewrite or edit some part of it, or all of it, and full disclosure I did try a couple of times. I thought, surely I can do better if I really try hard to write something else. But that's the thing, sometimes it ain't about effort, it's about instinct. And knowing when to let your instinct have free rein and when to put your shoulder into it, is an art form all of its own. One I can't pretend I have always been particularly good at discerning.

It is only the atoms of us that live forever, what is made from them does not. Only those smallest of things can be saved, nothing built from them can ever be saved, all they can ever do, is die. And so I start to imagine what the present day might look like, what now might feel like if I could find it. Are the past and the future both places we never really lived either? Are they just billions of nows piled up on top of each other? So is *now* where all of it lives? The past, the present and the future?

I can't pretend that I fully understand all the words that arrived that day for 'Never Really Tire' but the best songs often arrive without one's summoning or requirement. You're just a vessel to be poured into. Just get out of the way. It's the getting out of one's own way that can be the tricky bit. Especially for me, given I have spent so much of my life standing smack bang in the middle of it. Songs can evaporate when noticed, like a meditative state that's noticed pops the bubble of it. 'No mind', they say in Buddhism. That can work for songwriting too. Sometimes. And other times you have to graft and craft until you've gone quite round the bend. Believe me, I speak as someone who has at times taken five years to write one song. Mercifully though, not for this album.

I still have that dream sometimes. It arrives in the day more than the night. I'll fall to it from my chair. Into the sky through the floor. The forest below crashing, rising and foaming like a wild storm at sea. Every shade of green writhing and billowing in the tempest. At times in the dream I am the eagle again, sometimes a crow, but mostly I am just a man, falling in time.

ALBUM THEME 2

Home

September 2022

'And Belfast continues, never doubted it wouldn't
It's climbed off the canvas more than any other city
could've'

From 'This Is the Sound of Your Voice'

The coastal path between Belfast and Bangor is drawn by a genial but unsteady hand. It wends its way between our oldest and newest cities with a playfulness and lack of hurry not built by, or for, the modern world. As the path follows the coastline pretty faithfully you could say it was forged more by geology and ancient forces than the folks that would eventually lay the path down so we, the non-hunter-gatherers in all our dainty ways, might walk it. The first human settlers in this corner of our island would have hugged this coastline without need of a path, foraging and hunting along here, the thought of a leisurely stroll never entering their minds. What species of thing would walk for pleasure and not necessity? From those first settlers thousands of years ago to me looking at my watch at 11:26 a.m. right now today, a lot has happened in this place. On this island.

Jan Carson in her extraordinary novel *The Firestarters* said Belfast 'is like a square from one side and a circle from the other. You could go blind staring at it.' Religion, politics, geography, borders, fathers, sons. We have fought between ourselves for at least a millennium, depending on when in time you fire the starter pistol/first shot. But I never wanted a fight. That's why I ran from here when I was 18. I ran because I didn't understand any of it. Didn't understand the anger and hate. I had my own anger which I barely understood so I sure as hell wasn't gonna pile the anger of a thousand years on top of it. So away I went. Blinded perhaps by the naivety of youth and not knowing yet that there is anger everywhere in the world, but also there is wonder everywhere. And usually you will find whichever one you go looking for, be that in the place you were born or five thousand miles away. I realised way too late in life that it was not a *place* I was running from, it was myself.

When away though, it wasn't too long before I started to feel the pull of here on my soul. A pull that suggested the land of my birth had never actually been disconnected from my heart at all. Whatever it was I didn't understand about this place it seemed this place understood me, in a way I still find hard to explain, or even comprehend. And all that running I did seemed like it was always on the end of an elastic that would eventually reach its limit and, rather than snap, would begin to inexorably pull me back home. Towing me from continents and oceans away.

I'm one bay over from my house on the coastal path and the weather has turned. Mark Twain once said of New England, if you don't like the weather wait five minutes. This is also very much true of Bangor, the weather dial over my hometown always stuck on the setting – 'yes'. The sun was splitting the sky when I left the house and, not ten minutes since I closed the front door behind me, the rain has started, hard, as if it's trying to make a point. If you're gonna leave the house, Lightbody, you better bring all your clothes with you in a bag. What do you mean you didn't bring your dad's old fishing waders?! To round off this meteorological shithousery, the tide is in and, at each zenith, fully occupies both beach and path. I can either turn back or try to dance my way between tidal peaks and troughs on my tiptoes play-ing a game of low-stakes Russian roulette where the only potential bullet in the gun is wet feet, oh yeah, and of course the bad mood that accompanies waterlogged shoes. On occa-sion, after today on this same walk during high tide, I will stand high on the bluff overlooking the beach and take my socks and shoes off, wade through the tide and then put my shoes back on further up the path. But I don't think of that today so I try to dance across the lip of the tide. Forgetting of course that I can't dance. So now with shoes spilling over with sea water I slosh up the path to higher ground and think about all the times in my life I thought way too late to take the high road, or indeed, way too late to just give up and turn back.

As I drag my wet feet to elevation I think about yesterday when I was driving up to the Lisburn Road on the other side of Belfast. I realised there is a moment on the M3 when you are in a kind of triple state of being; all at once you are going around, going through, and also hanging over Belfast all at the same time, and if you peer over and into the city from this trifecta you can see the higgledy-piggledy wildness and apparent lack of planning of the great city's construction. Or should I say reconstruction? And it can seem from this vantage that you could drive right over it like it means nothing, and you wouldn't, or couldn't, possibly know what this city has gone through.

There is a baked-in tangledness to Belfast. A city built out of the wreckage of itself again and again. A world war thumped fire onto it and then a war with itself tried hard to finish it off, tearing it down to the studs so many damn times it is hard to imagine how a place could abide so much open-heart surgery. Or indeed recover from it.

You could argue this both ways but, in having to rebuild, reinvent, restart itself so many times, would it ever be possible for Belfast to know itself, or conversely does it know itself better than most other places on earth because it knows, so intimately, fire and pain and vengeance and forgiveness and regret and redemption? It has seen its own insides, and knows them far too well. Its viscera still visible now, pink and fierce. To walk in Belfast you get the feeling sometimes you are trudging through its turned-out guts, its heart beating on top of you so loud it is at times all you can hear.

But that's the thing, the heart still beats. Loud and strong. A city that wouldn't die, holding in its battered innards a people that wouldn't give in.

Something used to happen to me in those streets that never really happens to me anywhere else. I get lost, like a lot. I have a reputation among my friends that I have a bad sense of direction, but when I really think about it I have to disagree, as there are plenty of cities I've only been a handful of times and can find my way fine. But the streets of Belfast, in a city I have known most of my life, I'd somehow find myself lost almost every time I walk them. Maybe a friend is with me, usually Davy, and I'll turn to them and ask, 'Which way now, mate?' and they'll laugh and roll their eyes and say, 'Same way it always is, mate.' Was the city playing a trick on me? Did it think of me as an interloper? Too often gone. A deserter.

It had always kinda made me sad though. That I didn't know the way in our capital, or perhaps it didn't want me to know it. The place seemed to keep me at arm's length. Maybe the streets would shift around at night and when I would return, they'd whisper to themselves, 'Look at the state of him, he has no fucking clue where he is.' But what I didn't realise until more recently was that it was trying to teach me something. Something my father had tried to teach me long ago. If you don't know the place where you are from, how can you really know anywhere else? In these last ten years or so this city has begun to unlock for me. Northern Ireland is a significant part of the map of my heart; Belfast was perhaps a piece of that heart-map that simply needed to be drawn. Either by me, or by the city itself. Or we drew it together.

We find our home when we find it. Sometimes we are born into it and we don't know any different and don't wanna know. And that is perfectly fine. To be born into a place and die in a place and in between feel like that place is yours, that it belongs to you – what a beautiful thing if that's what you want. For some though, maybe me, home is harder to define, or to find. I went looking for mine and my wanderlust took me everywhere. And I found some places that felt an awful lot like home along the way. And I'm grateful, eternally grateful, to all those places. And they may well call back to me in years to come. Naguib Mahfouz said, 'Home is not where you are born; home is where all your attempts to escape cease.' Maybe I am simply no longer trying to escape.

The rain continues to pile down and most of Belfast Lough seems to be tumbling out of my shoes. There may in fact be fish swimming around in there. I cut a rather miserable-looking figure and just as I reach peak woe-is-me there is a sonic boom of thunder and I laugh, at the weather and at myself. I like it when I catch myself wallowing. Because enough of that. The thunder and the laughter mix in me and the cocktail they make tastes a lot like humility and I give in to the elements and let the fish swim in my shoes and the rain baptise me. I think of the person that taught me humility and in an instant I have swum from the North Down coast across the province to Fountain Street in NI's maiden city. Called Derry by some, Londonderry by some, the birthplace of my mother, and our Johnny too. I arrive years ago in the house of my grandmother.

My nana's laugh echoes upwards through the deep channel of the old terraced house all the way to the attic room where me and Sarah and the other grandkids are always billeted when we stay here. The adults downstairs invent new sounds as we hang over the balcony and long to understand what those sounds mean and why they're all so darn funny. My mum has four sisters and two brothers so this house is always full to the brim, us little ones almost spilling out of the skylight at the top of the house.

It's coming up to Christmas 1984. It's the day my dad would die on 35 years from now but we don't know that yet. Is the ghost of him trapped inside the echo of his laughter as it climbs the stairs of the house? My nana's laugh follows his up here too. In my memory I hear her laugh clearer than my father's. She is always laughing in my memory.

Rebecca Wray was one of those women. Touched by the divine. In a country in the middle of a civil war her door was defiantly always open. A devout Protestant, it never stopped her from a lifelong best friendship with Margaret Monaghan, a Catholic. To those that didn't grow up in Norn Iron in those days it may seem like no big deal, but it was. A very big deal. Rebecca's door would be open for Protestants and Catholics alike, and anyone else for that matter, and people would come from all over Derry for a cup of tea with Betty, as they all called her. If there is any kind of soul in me, any kind of goodness, any semblance of decency, it has been put there by her and my mother.

When she dies 16 years from now, it will be the first death in the family I am old enough to understand. At the funeral I will read the Bible passage we know she was reading when she passed because the book was found open at it on her chest, and neither my mum nor my aunts and uncles were in any fit state to read it themselves. And after I was done reading, I joined them in their tears. So I had tears for my grandmother. That is why, when they don't come for my father, I will feel like there is something rotted inside me.

I really don't know what I believe but my dear friend Gabrielle, herself one of the few truly great healers I have ever known, took me to a reading once by a Chinese woman who had escaped the Maoist purge of such sages in China in the 1960s. When I walked into the room I didn't say a word. Not a word. I was asked nothing and I offered nothing. I was ushered to sit down in front of her. You can believe me or not, I barely believe it sometimes and I was there, but the following is simply what happened on that day. She took my hand and said, 'There is a wolf on your left' (I had always felt the presence of a wolf, I don't know why, but I did, so her words already had me holding my breath a little). 'And on your right, there's a woman with a radiant smile, she says she loves you and is always there protecting you. Her name is Rebecca.'

Approaching Bangor on the coastal path and the sun comes out as if in a mad rush. You'd need to see it for yourself because you'd think it was something artificial, from *The Truman Show* maybe, but the rain just stops. Like a parkour runner leaping at full pelt onto the top of a single beam on only one foot and somehow, defying both gravity and momentum, just stops, dead. I think I can actually see the last raindrop hit the ground in the tiniest of full stops. Or perhaps it was just falling out of sync with all its other raindrop pals and they chided him, 'Ah for fuck's sake, Trev, late again.' Well, Trev hits the ground and the sun riots out on his cue and immediately blinds all the wildlife including me by bouncing off the water-made mirror of the path and into our eyes like skimmed stones of light. Birds fly into trees, bears fall down manholes, giraffes walk into walls, lions bump into each other and say 'excuse me' in posh accents. OK, so none of that last bit happened but I imagine it does. Does that count? No, you say. OK. Fair dos.

Now I'm walking along the edge of Bangor marina and my ears catch a handful of words cookie-cut from a passing conversation. Just these eight words: 'See all them yachts, all the money people?' I chuckle gently inwardly so as not to let on I just heard the elderly woman and be outed as an eavesdropper. The worst kind of dropper. I think of all the times people must have heard non-sequiturs from my passing conversations and my stomach does a loop. But there was such sweetness to the tone of her voice and it leaves me with a smile. Plus she's right, see all them yachts …

The marina sits in the same exact spot where stood the black-sand beach of the Bangor of my childhood, long before all the money people and their yachts. The five-year-old me, 40-some years ago, could have made a castle then with that thick cementy sand and, if it weren't for the marina being flung over it since then, that sandcastle would still be sitting there today, proud as punch. Where did they put that sand when they took the beach? We could've rebuilt Bangor seafront with it. It's been in need of a facelift for a while.

The Guillemot cafe looks out over the old side of Bangor Harbour. The side that hasn't changed at all since I were a lad. The side I used to fish off with my mates. We'd cycle down on our BMXs with our rods and gear and fish for hours off the pier. There'd always been hushed talk of some fella catching a conger eel in the honeycomb layers of the sea-facing side of the pier. They would lurk in there, the congers, waiting for lads to fall in and they'd drag you down into their lairs. Take your hand off, some guy too old to be scaring kids would say. Take your arm off. Swallow you whole they could. The stories would get more and more outlandish and we would believe them all. 'Stevie caught one two days ago, didn't you Stevie?' Stevie would nod and immediately become our new hero. The king of the pier. He caught a conger you know, did Stevie. It would grow in the retelling. Three foot, four foot, six foot, ten foot. None of us at that age really knowing how big any of those measurements were, but there would be oohs and aahs and Stevie would be coronated and be-sceptred, and various oil paintings of King Stevie were commissioned and hung in the gallery of our minds. All hail King Stevie! The conger slayer. Ten-foot congers would swim around in my dreams with Jaws, circling the great shark like a force field shaped like DNA strands. I genuinely saw one caught once just off the pier. When its gigantic prehistoric head breached the water, I never wanted to be further away from myself in my short life.

In the Guillemot I take a seat and my book out. Louise Kennedy's *Trespasses*, a masterpiece I am near the end of. I open it where I left off and in seconds it glues me back in. Everything is great about this wee cafe. The people that work here and the food and the feeling I get sitting on my own reading in the town I was born in, the feeling of belong-ing. I went around the whole world many many times to find my way back here to discover it was where I belonged all this time. Where all my attempts to escape finally ceased.

Later I will do the same journey along the coast in reverse and make my way back to my house. I'll think about all the journeys I have taken on this island, north, south, east and west and imagine all the journeys I still want to make. I'll think about how I don't know this place, and also that this is the only place I know well. I'll think about you and how I have so much to tell you of how far I have gone, and how I found my way back home. It was likely, right from the start, that my life was going to throw me out into the world and haul me back just in time for so many things. But I was just too late for you.

JACK

Part Two

21 December 2019

It's the next day and Belfast Lough has me held in its freezing December arms. As I swim a heron glides past with no effort at all mere inches from the surface. The water today is so still and waveless that the massive bird's reflection is perfectly trapped tight under the sea. Makes me think there is a mirror-world flipped and beneath ours in which the sky is the sea and the sea is the sky. Where we breathe the water and drink the air. Where all the birds swim and all the fish fly. But in which everything is doomed to be naught but mimics of their above-world counterparts. Every detail copied. Every movement matched. If I raise my hand, they raise their hand. If I run, they run. If I swing a hammer, they swing a hammer. If my father dies, their father dies. And I couldn't stop it for them, just like I couldn't stop it for me.

And even if I stand so perfectly still so as not to make a single error or ripple in the world it won't matter because all that happens then is that they are buried in the rubble of my stillness.

My mind is numb. My heart is numb. My body though, as I'm definitely aware of the cold water, seems not. So it at least works. This buoys my spirit a little. To be aware of functionality, even on some base level, is to be functional on some base level. Some atom of functionality just enough to prove concept. At the very least as much as the Tin Man in *The Wizard of Oz*. If I only had a heart though. I shall go looking for it later. It's around here somewhere. I never really think about my organs on a good day but now, neck deep in a lucid sea, I imagine my insides hollow. The windswept streets of an abandoned village. A stray dog looking for scraps in the crossroads of my neck and shoulder. Stores still stocked but maybe some cans strewn on the shop floors, bringing the observer to the realisation that everyone left in a hurry. And that something horrible happened here.

The moon is up already trying to hurry the winter sun. Makes me think of a wee dog, like a Jack Russell, trying to bully a big dog like a Great Dane. The Great Dane unmoved, detached, patient. The Jack Russell, nipping and yelping to no avail. The sun'll set when it sets, and not before. This is Northern Ireland in the winter though, so it'll be soon, the hours of darkness easily outnumbering the daylight hours two to one this time of year. To sleep in during the Irish winter is to know regret on a cellular level. 'You'll miss the best part of the day,' my dad says, looking down on me from some fragment of free-floating time. Even more pertinent in the winter months for it is also the *only* part of the day. Everything else being night. One sliver of light caught between two hulking expanses of darkness. Today I did my damnedest to miss that scant sliver so I'll have to make do with what's left. So I watch the moon bite the ankles of the sun from the mirror of the sea and know somewhere below me is another me breathing the salt water and swimming in the sky.

As cold as this sea is it won't freeze and snap yesterday from my skin and bones and so it hangs on me like so much scaffolding. The type of scaffolding that if it went up next door you'd think, 'Shit, that's gonna be a long one,' and you'd brace for a year's worth of banging and sawing and drilling and hammering. I take the hint and brace for prolonged construction.

I wonder how you dealt with your own father's death. He was gone before I was born. You never talked about it. Or did I never ask you about it? Another holstered question. I'll add it to the list. Maybe you, like me, wondered how the biggest man of all the men in your life was brought so low. Did he also tower above you so vast that he blocked out the sun, and in his absence was the sunlight suddenly too blinding to see anything else? I'm falling again, this time down through the water, and I come up in our kitchen three decades ago. I look 14 maybe but I'm as tall then as I am now, so I could be a bit older. I was too tall for the wrong part of my life. At school, when all I wanted was to be invisible, I was six foot plus and built of twigs. Here I am though, in our kitchen and my mum and I are in the middle of a heated exchange. Dad is off camera, his eyes likely to be in the paper as usual, his ears though are beginning to tune in to the argument. It ends in a climax. I tell my mum to fuck off. It is the first time I have ever sworn at either of them. Time stops with a thud. I am suddenly aware of my own heartbeat. It shakes its head at me and says, 'Jeez, I wouldn't have said that'. 'No shit,' my brain says back to it. My mouth, the culprit, now has nothing to say for itself. 'Ah, you're clamped now, aren't you?' my heart and brain say in unison. Clamped it is. My dad has risen from his chair after putting his newspaper down with a care that feels like a harbinger of the impending opposite of care. Unable to think of anything else to do I run away.

Up the stairs two at a time to my room and I take the roof-space pole and jam it under my door handle checking its secureness and feeling confident I have made the room an impenetrable fortress. OK, he can't get in. I stand for a moment not quite knowing what to do with myself. Hands in pockets, then folded, then hanging at my sides like weights. My dad has never hit us but he's shouted plenty. So for him to be so quiet was enough for me to immediately realise this is not like any time before and shit could be about to kick off. I'm inventing a time machine in my head to go back and hold my hand over my mouth before 'fuck off' spilled out of it. My imagination is overloaded though, and can't invent much else past the DeLorean from *Back to the Future*. Signals are coming at me from the engine room of my imagination, yelling: what do you expect from us, we're too busy at the moment for anything new, we have enough on our plate trying to imagine all the ways your six foot two father who's built like a tank is gonna kick fuck outta you, we've drawn diagrams for that if you want to see those. The rest of the inner mind's office doors have 'Gone fishing' signs pinned to them, still swinging from recent evacuation. His footsteps are on the stairs now. Slow and deliberate. It's a scene cribbed from every horror movie ever made. Now he's at the door and before I can even take a lungful of breath he has opened it in one fluid motion, the roof-space pole shattering into a thousand pieces. The fragments land on my head and clothes. This really happened. He really opened the door like that. Like it was nothing. Like it was just a door to be opened. No obstruction or obstacle. One swing through with his arm. Everything that was meant to hold was obliterated. I am terrified. I can see the look on my face in my memory because I saw the look on his when he realised he had fright-ened me so thoroughly. The red mist of his anger fell away immediately. His only words, 'Go and apologise to your mother.' You better believe I go and say sorry to mum, still dusted with the roof-space pole we used to have.

This man, this giant, how can he be the same man I saw yesterday? How can he be the same man of these last eight years withering, then obliterated by a ceaseless, ravenous monster of a disease that I wouldn't wish on a single solitary soul.

I pull my frozen legs through and out of the water and traipse up the beach to my clothes. The low winter sunset throws the shadows long across the sand. My own shadow thin, anorexic even, trailing behind me like a hungry stray dog begging to be fed. The exaggerated length of it gives the impression it's trying to get away from me. Glancing back I swear I clock it making a shape that does not mimic mine. That we are somehow not in sync. Or that it is not in fact my shadow after all. Perhaps the shadow of something else that follows me now, and only visible in the dying light of the day, or just the dying. Whoever or whatever this apparition might be it seems to have clicked back into lockstep with me and the two of us dry ourselves and put our clothes back on.

The seagulls and crows on the beach make word-like sounds, talking to me, in their caws and clicks, as though old friends. We banter back and forth for a little while, me trying to remember a rhyme but after a while realising it might actually be for magpies anyway. 'Do not go in there', I hear one of the crows say. What? And where? Where should I not go in? Plead as I might the little guy gives no further context. I must be hearing things. I've heard tell that happens in loss.

Seeing things too. Things like shadows coming unstuck from their moorings, or avian prophesies perhaps, or, in the weeks and months to come, your face in crowds, everywhere. I've heard that can happen. I'll come to know it happens, soon enough.

The next day we will go back to the funeral home to see you for the last time. The three of us lined up outside the door behind which you are lying in state puts me in mind of every Christmas morning when we were growing up. We'd line up outside the living-room door: eldest, so you, first, then mum, then me, then Sarah. Her and I at this point unhinged with excitement at what Santa may have left behind him. In we would go to find Star Wars or Barbie waiting on the floor beneath the tree and we would be the happiest we would be all year, until the first fight of course. My sister was my first verbal sparring partner. It was a boot camp for the wars of words to come with you. We would make every effort to find a way between us to try to ruin Christmas, at least for a few hours. So here we are again lined up outside a door at Christmas, but just three of us now, with all the excitement, energy and fission vacuumed out of the moment and sealed somewhere. Our mum likely has it stored away in Tupperware, labelled neatly: all future possible Christmas joy. To be clicked open some years hence maybe, if we don't forget about it in the freezer. Though I do know how lucky I was to have so many good Christmases before this one. That is never lost on me. We press on through the door that none of us want to walk through, my sister's hand on my mum's shoulder and mine on hers like some sad, slow conga line.

The room is stillness. Nothing but stillness. It takes me a moment to be brave enough to lift my head up to look at you, hoping maybe that when I do it won't be you. That there's been a mistake. 'We gave him two aspirin and he was right as rain,' the funeral parlour lady says. 'We stuck him in a taxi home.' The thought makes me feel immediately terrible, because if that were true then we would now be standing in the exact same spot borrowing some other poor family's terrible day. We might pass them in the corridor on the way out, awkward and noddingly apologetic but the three of us filled so quickly to the brim with relief we can do nothing but dump all our unused grief onto them in some slow, cruel drive-by and bugger off out the door. I look up finally. It's you. Fuck.

All the colours that lived in your face, the pinks, the blotchy reds, the oranges, have moved out and only grey remains. There is though, a dark blue tinge around your lips. Makes me think of the blue Slush Puppie drinks (in America, they call them snow cones) we would have at Dundonald Ice Bowl when we were kids, the times you would take us. Ice skating looks effortless on the telly during the Winter Olympics. Twirls, jumps, spins and the carving of great shapes out of bombastic slices of classical music. Professional, and very regular, skaters make it look like they were born with skates on and they fly on the ice with great skill and grace and elegance. Ice skating twice a year though, the lowest-tier practitioner, the once-in-a-whiler, was a great way to do grievous bodily harm to yourself, and an almost guaranteed way to get rid of any unwanted dignity you wished to offload. It likely would've been better, and faster, and probably warmer if someone would have just taken a cricket bat to me in the car park. My dad could skate though. For a big man he was surprisingly graceful. An athlete in his youth, the captain of every sports team at his school, he had a way of making things look easy sometimes. I did not inherit much of that athleticism. Decent enough on a good day at a couple of sports but a million miles from gifted, not like him. And ice skating was just not my jam. In the times between visits to the ice rink though, I would forget this and work myself up into what looked an awful lot like excitement to go back. Much like when I have sat behind a drum kit over the years and I would forget I had never learned the drums in the first place and not practised in the meantime, but every single time there is a wee moment before I pick up the drumsticks when I think, 'This time, I'm gonna be great at the drums.' There's no logic to it but it's true, every time I sit behind a kit, just like every time I lace up a pair of ice skates, that's what I think. This time! Obviously, what happens next sounds like a guy falling down a staircase with drums gaffer-taped to his body, and my little fantasy bubble gets popped right quick. Same with skating, just with even more falling.

So after landing on my hands, knees, face, arse and elbows enough times I would sit on the sidelines in a huff watching my dad and my sister who were having a whale of a time, and I would paint my face with the blue Slush Puppie my dad had got me as a bribe to sit down and shut up and give his head peace for ten minutes. I was twenty-six. Only kidding, I was eight. And that's a Peter Kay joke, but in my head now is every effort to try and avoid what is right in front of me. Perhaps hoping that if I can take myself to you in my memory, I can bring you back with me when I return.

But I know nothing I do can make up for any of it. This moment more than any other so far makes me very aware of that. Goodbyes are said to you by the two women. I stay in the room after they leave. 'It's just you and me now kid,' you used to say to me. I don't know if I say this out loud, but I think it pretty loudly. I'm so afraid to touch you but, against every instinct, I do reach my hand up to your face and touch your forehead; the closer I get I feel dragged towards you, along with all light and gravity, like an event horizon. I have been in the Irish Sea in winter, I have swum in (even colder) Irish lakes in January, I have been in ice baths in Russian spas, I have had cold showers on minus 17 Chicago mornings. I never though, in my life, felt a cold like you are now. There is a burn still on my hand from it, and whether or not it is real, it feels real to me. That touch on your forehead scarred across my palm forever. When I think of it my hand throbs with the Arctic shivering sting held in all that remained of you. On the beach me and probably my shadow are dressed now and I'm looking back towards the water and it's the seagulls this time that are the more talkative. They are advising me like ancient sages or oracles. They tell me, 'Don't wait till it's too late. Say everything now that you have always wanted to say. Apologise to him. Ask him all the things you have always wanted to know. Tell him you are glad that he is your father and that you love him.' 'He died yesterday,' I say in response. 'Oh, never mind then,' the seagulls say, 'you're too late.' And they bend their golden beaks into the wind, their wings curved like saddles and they go find some other person to give the same advice to, a person with a living father. A crow hops over, I wait for it to give me some hopefully more helpful advice, he hops away again without saying a word.

The first full day without a father is surprisingly much like any other day. Talking to seagulls and crows, hallucinating up-to-no-good shadows, pondering death on a beach, y'know Saturdays, am I right? I feel tied to something yet also soaring. Not like a bird, regal, uncontained, unbound by gravity or logic, with their somehow natural, mystical flight. What sorcery is that? What alchemy? Turning feathers and sheer will into levitation. No, that's not me. I feel elevated but restrained. Held in suspension slightly above the surface of the earth, but way too tightly. So not a bird, more like a kite. Not so free as one would imagine is the kite. Not as much as it might appear. Hanging on the wind's every word looks an awful lot like flying, but being tethered is the very opposite of flight. There's a kite on the next beach over, reigning over the wind as if a king, held in a moment of majesty and weightlessness, but then as it gets abruptly tugged to the lefthand side by its controller it remembers it is not free after all. The wind, rejecting the controller's suggestion, dumps the kite down hard on its nose. Yep, a kite, it's a kite I'm feeling like, not a bird.

Wherever you are. If there is a land beyond this one, and from it you have access to this land still, I don't want you to think I'm unhappy. I'm not. There is a future where the burned-down forest of you regrew from your atoms, and though all the plants and trees are different now there is at least life again.

The moon finally gets its way and no longer has to share the sky. I watch it lord it over the night from my window. So insistent was the moon today, so impatient, cocky, and yet its light does not even exist. It's playing with house money. It is a mirage, a mere reflection of the sun. So even though it has hurried it away it still has to borrow the sun's light, which now bounces off the moon's smug face. There are ships at anchor in Belfast Lough and the moon-mirrored sunlight falls between them, its sword-like shape cutting into the dark waters of the bay. I think of the men and women on those ships and feel myself lucky, I can't think of anything worse than being at sea. Then I feel shame when I don't answer immediately to my mind asking me whether or not I would exchange a life at sea for a living father. 'Yes,' I say, but a beat late. My mind has already taken my hesitation as my first answer and I hop on the ride of kicking the shit out of myself for being the worst. This is a daily ride so you'd think I would be a seasoned driver by now. But I am not. Still on my learner's permit.

There is a ferry in the water escaping the lough. Heading to Scotland no doubt. I think of all the times I rode that ferry over to university in Dundee and back and the handful of times we took it to a holiday in England or Scotland in the caravan. Ah the caravan. Hell on wheels. Mostly it was Ireland we explored with it fastened onto the tow bar of our ugly brown Volvo or ugly green Peugeot. Whatever car my dad chose he made sure the colour was ugly. It's as if he went into the dealership and the salesman started to say, 'Good after-noon, sir, as you can see, we have a great selection of fantastic cars ...' 'Ap ap ap,' my father interjects, cutting him off right quick, 'that's all well and good but where are your butt-ugly cars? Let me see those ones.' 'Yes sir,' the salesman kinda hesi-tant but obliging, '*those ones* are out the back ...' (subtext: where no one can see them). That makes it sound like we had an array of cars. We didn't. We had two over the 18 years I lived at home. Both as ugly as any cars I have ever seen since the invention of the automobile. So, depending on the year, whichever of the two ugly cars it was driving us on our two-week holiday there was always a caravan attached to it.

The abiding sound of those holidays in Ireland was a relentless deluge of rain beating down like machine-gun fire on the caravan's plastic roof, with us playing cards, barely able to hear ourselves think, daydreaming about our friends that were sitting on Algarve beaches or dangling their skis from Alpine lifts. We'd be driving through Ireland, me and my sister trying to drown out a running commentary of the history of whatever county we were trundling through from our incorrigible father, with Iron Maiden or Metallica blasting full belt on our Walkmans. He'd pepper his lectures with his catchphrase, 'You can't know the world until you know your own island.' Us in the back drawing up borders and battle plans should either one of us so much as breathe in the other's direction. 'Mum, Sarah's on my side!' 'No I'm not mum, Gary's on my side!' 'Will you two for god's sake behave!' It was all about sides in those days. My sister and I playing out in microcosm what was going on in the streets of Belfast and Derry and beyond. We stopped short of shooting each other, but I think only because we didn't have access to weapons.

Thing is, I am so glad now that he showed us our island. I may have rolled my eyes and only half listened but I saw most of Ireland north, south, east and west. It was sewn into me on those trips so I wouldn't forget it, its endless green patchworks stitched over my heart for safe keeping. The love I have now for the whole island I was born on, its people and their music, art, creativity, mischievousness and magic was fostered on those trips. That was all him. Mainly cause none of the rest of us wanted to go anywhere in the bloody caravan, so if it was up to us, we'd be in the south of France. The fact that we could never have afforded a foreign holiday never occurred to us. Dad, knowing he couldn't give us France or Spain, was just trying to give us some kind of holiday. Ungrateful wee fuckers we were.

So we've landed at a campsite by a beach somewhere on the west coast of Ireland. In my memory of it the sun is always setting. It's no wonder really, given what happened, but this minute now is streaked through with sunlight, fanned out across the dying summer evening. The year is 1983. Pip and Kim were my dad's dogs when we were born. They were there before us. How do I know that? Well, because my dad was fond of reminding us. You see I was allergic to animal hair, something they found out when they brought me home and my eyes swelled up and I had some trouble drawing breath. So the dogs were moved out to the garage, into a cosy kennel built for them by my dad. And when my sister and I ever acted up, which was often, he would say, 'Yous can move into the garage and I'll bring the dogs back in here.' He was half joking. Remembering that the other half of that wasn't a joke at all. The two dogs were divine so it was easy to see why he would be in favour of swapping us out for them. Kim a sweet-natured yellow Lab, and Pip a brown and white bundle of endless energy and fun in the shape of a springer spaniel. God, we loved that wee dog, me and my sister. My dad was a gundog trainer and those two dogs were highly trained and expert in retrieving recently shot wildfowl. As kids though, we just wanted to play with them. We did not know the ceaseless throwing of tennis balls to fetch would ruin a gundog. Kim was never that interested in our shenanigans, but Pip. Oh Pip loved to fetch and run and play. He was a sprite. A spirit from another dimension. Long summer nights he'd be out in the garden with us, my dad shouting 'Stop throwing that bloody ball for that dog, you'll wreck him.' But how could we not? Sure, it was the best fun ever, and he thought so too. I still see that wee dog from time to time. He took up a place in my heart when he passed. Chasing tennis balls around in there, happy as anything.

My sister, mum and I were all in or around the caravan watching my dad stride through the sunbeams back from walking the dogs on the beach. But there was only the one dog with him. My dad looked as distraught as I had ever seen him. He said nothing to us and the two adults conferred quietly for a moment and if I heard anything of that conversation it has been cobbled together from the fragments that I may have overheard or by stories I have been told since, but I got the gist. Pip, bless his wee bouncing heart, had crawled onto a sand dune, curled up in a ball and let out his last breath. The world fell apart. Our Pip, gone. How? What? We didn't want to understand. And then, way too soon for us, as we hadn't caught up properly with the adults yet, there was talk of burying him. Here! But he'll be so far away from us! But he'll be lonely! We, my sister and I, whined and whinged and moaned that we needed to bring him home to bury him in the back garden so he'll be near us and he won't be alone. My dad finally acquiesced to our demand, likely just out of the attrition we wrought down on him, and for a quieter life. So we packed up the campsite, hooked up the caravan, put poor Pip in the boot of the car and drove all the way home through the winding, awful roads that cut across Ireland from west to east back in those days. No motorways or highways. Just car-sickening, winding roads. When home, my dad set to digging a hole for Pip as we wept and were of no help at all. And we put him in the hole and covered it over and got a little breeze block and painted his name on it and set it in the ground to look over him. And though it is no longer our garden he rests there still.

What I did not know because you never showed it, and only found out much later on from my mum, was that your heart was broken. Clean snapped in two at the loss of your beloved dog. You let us have the space to feel and show our emotions and did not let any of your own spill out and land anywhere near us. You only wanted to bury him there on the west coast of Ireland because you couldn't bear to bring him home, dead in the car. But you drove all the way home with him anyway because we asked you to, through those windy wee roads, with your heart sunk a foot down in your chest in two broken pieces.

If you ever were wondering, looking on at us now from whatever land you rest in, what man I see when I think of you, what version of you strides through my memories, it is him. That man is the man you are to me. A man who would endure the long and winding roads of his desolation just because we asked you to. I only wish I thanked you for it.

ALBUM THEME 3
Love (Part One)

Love in Two Directions

Maybe, how the hell would I know, but maybe the meaning of life is love in two directions.

Outwards towards others.

Inwards towards oneself.

And, most importantly, the balance between the two.

But finding that balance between the two ... there lies the magic. Not getting stuck in the middle of the pivot between the two, stuck on some bankrupt liminal space, caught as if on fly paper, so you can't love anything at all, no not that. Rather ebbing and flowing like the tides, feeling into when you are being called to be of service to others, to love others, or at least to try to understand them, and when you are being called to be of service to yourself, to love yourself, or at least to try and understand yourself. There is a real danger though of getting stuck on either side. Love only yourself and you'll neglect, or even be of harm, to others. Love only others and you'll neglect yourself and eventually, ironically, be of no use to others.

It is a dance. A flow. A pendulum. And perhaps better to let love call to you, than to call out, like a wolf in the night, to it.

But I have never figured out how to do either very well. Too scared to love someone, or let them love me, and too many years battering myself from the inside to love much of anything I find in there. But in the brief glimpses I get into a world in which love is balanced, and swings in tune with the universe on some celestial pivot between the two states, I sense there are answers in there. The answers to every question imaginable. Most days though, I am just too afraid to see what it wants to show me, and I have pushed away all the love I was ever offered.

Love (Part Two)

I Just Don't Know How to Love

January 2024

This is indeed a strange type of drowning. A kind of drowning in wonder, like staring at a Rothko until your eyes melt, until you can feel your own heart trapped on, and beating within, the canvas in front of you. An artist now deceased somehow reading your mind in the present day, whispering into you some secret code of the universe. Calling back at you from decades, from centuries, from the beginning of life itself. You feel all of it, and none of it, because it is both too much to feel and impossible not to. To me anyway, this is a lot like falling in love. We are planted in the English countryside in Fraser T. Smith's extraordinary studio deep in the third week of recording this album. We have spent 20 years making records with the wonderful Jacknife Lee, who is a dear friend and mentor to us. We just wanted to try something different this time around. We were also now a three piece after being a five piece for so long, and while we have boundless love and respect for Jonny and Pablo for being on the journey with us all those amazing years we now have to try and figure out how to do it all, just the three of us. We'd tried once already to record the album in a different city with a new producer but it hadn't quite worked out as we would have liked. No one's fault, it just didn't click. So here we are again with Fraser and it clicked so loudly that I think we may all have gone temporarily deaf.

Fraser is full to the brim with sweet mischievous charm. Unflappable, serene and genial and everything feels fun and limitless under his auspices. Right from day one with him. Here we are on day, I dunno, 14 is it, and it still is. Never saw him lose his cool or his sense of fun once during the month we spent with him. And that's the thing, the first effort at recording this album took five months. With Fraser, the open energy flow he created, and his incredible engineer Scott, we had the record all done in five weeks. Ironic, I guess, for him to be so unhurried and yet somehow everything seemed to hurtle along at light speed.

Every time Nathan or Johnny picked up a guitar or sat behind a piano in this place something magical happened. Sounds like it was some drugged-up fairy tale that could not possibly be true. As someone who has done his fair share, and, most likely, your fair share of drugs, I assure you I know what being out of your mind feels like. We were in our minds, and our bodies, and it showed. Nate channelled his guitar in a way I don't think I've seen from him. Pure confidence in himself and such grace, and it was a beautiful thing to witness. And J plays anything to hand or he sits in front of, and did so all the way through this with an effortlessness and skill that was a joy to watch. Both J and Nate's whole hearts burst over everything they played. We were each there to see and hear everything the other two did. For the last few albums we all didn't show up every day. Life gets in the way sometimes during an album so it's understandable everyone might not be there every single day. But this time we were. Every day. This time Nate and J were witness to me. J and I were witness to Nate. Nate and I were witness to J. There is a pact that forms in that type of witnessing. One that never needs to be mentioned, but it creates an endless flow of energy and light between yous like the rolling infinity of a Möbius strip.

Not that it was five weeks of continual bliss, that was just Fraser; come to think of it he may have been on drugs. It was tough at times but nothing ever felt like a dead end. We would not allow ourselves to labour on something too long, relying on instinct more than graft. You can bury a record if you push too hard.

We are, in this moment now, trying to finish a song called 'All This Time', which would eventually be retitled

'Everything's Here and Nothing's Lost'. Some guitars are added by J and Nate and it is sounding great but there has always been something missing for me in the bridge section and we couldn't find a way to figure it out. Even though the song, including the verse and chorus lyrics, was all written together on that second day of writing, the bridge always felt unfinished. I'm leaning over my book trying to hurl words at the pages and I find myself thinking of the times I have been in love and how they ended and if I could've stopped it. The thought catches me like a hook and I am pulled through towards that day.

I arrive back to where I lived a while ago like a fist flung down on a desk with a thump and I'm straight into the middle of it. Our last argument. When all that was left of us was built more from silence than from words. Like the world inside of an atom, mostly empty space with a few scant pieces of debris floating around that we could call electrons, or protons, or neutrons, or some rattling semblance of the few things that we can still talk about. You say the final handful of words that are left and I hear breaking and it's a while before I realise it's coming from me. Inside, somewhere deep. Like the sound of a giant tanker running aground, or a glacier beginning to self-destruct in subdermal cannon volleys of barks and cracks. Love is blind they say, but the ending of love also brings with it a particular deafness that is as exquisite as it is annihilating. Perhaps the senses shut down as the body does everything to try to protect itself from harm and hurt. You told me it was over and then I didn't hear anything you said after that. When I realise this, I wonder are those last words stored in me somewhere, in some other of my senses to be replayed to my useless, currently ornamental, ears at a later date. Or are all my senses powering down to spare me the hurt? I assume asking you now to repeat everything you just said and I didn't hear would only hasten your exit and I'm still trying, even with powerplant shut-down protocols initiated, to find a way to stop all this. But I'm rooted and mute. So I just stand here, 195 pounds of mince. Mince with myxomatosis. More obstacle than man.

When I got in the way of his telly my dad used to say, 'Son, you're a better door than a window,' and here I am a door again. Closed. Rusted at the hinges. Cobwebbed over. Almost impossible to open without a bloody good shove. And I'm still dumb and quicksanded when you walk out. In so many of the moments in which you must have felt unloved by me there was a sonorous, imploring voice inside my head screaming at me to tell you how I felt. That I loved you. That I understood you. That I saw you. I just didn't know how to say any of it out loud so as you could hear it. That voice was screaming that day too, telling you not to leave. That voice though couldn't achieve escape velocity because of the gravi-tational pull of my cowardice. So nothing of importance ever makes it all the way up to, and out of, my dumb, terrified mouth. And today that same dumb mouth is stuck shut again.

Merely decorative, a perfect match for my ears. I make a reminder to my future self: pick up milk, sugar, eggs, relearn to talk, ham, butter, be better than this for fuck's sake, bread, potatoes ...

So in the end we were like water evaporating on the surface of a hot clay pot, a strange shape diminishing, ever decreasing, and eventually no sign we were ever really there in the first place.

And what am I now? Just what I was before you: me. Me, and that's it? God knows me ain't good enough for anyone. Even myself.

Then, from this distance of so much time I replay the tape and watch it all happen again from your perspective. I look distant, uncaring, remote. A planet that has decided to orbit your sun from far too far away and got itself demoted to exoplanet. My arms are folded. I look everywhere but at you: the floor, my shoes, the shelf that I never got around to fixing. I don't respond to anything you're saying. I see it all now. It is as if a new part of my memory has unlocked after a decade or two. FBI files now un-redacted and available to the general public.

All this time and distance can show so much, but even though I can reach into this memory and watch it all again from your viewpoint I still can't reach into myself in that moment to spark my voice awake and say what was always in there, trapped. And I feel the distance pulling at me like some decades-long rope and now, as if in slow motion, am being hauled back up to the surface of the present day, gaining speed as I'm dragged through time by the scruff.

Back on the couch in Fraser's studio it likely looked like I'd nodded off. Did I? Maybe. Felt real. We are working on the elusive bridge of 'Everything's Here and Nothing's Lost'. We have tried to fill that bridge with all kinds of things. AHs, LAs, OHs, all the basic food groups. I am kicking around a melody and start scribbling words onto the face of it.

Maybe I love you like the ocean ...

'OK, that's a start,' I think. I'm cross-legged on the floor trying to bend the words out of me. Sometimes this helps. Sometimes nothing helps.

Like the ocean loves the sky ...

I had scribbled something else about this a while back. I check my notes. The horizon. No? Something else. Reaching. That was it. The ocean can never reach up and touch the sky.

Never gonna find a way to reach you
No matter how I try.

OK, now what else?

Maybe I can love you like the mountain ...

What? What the fuck does the mountain love? The snow, I guess.

Like the mountain loves the snow ...

How is that love? It is love to stop hurrying someone and give them the freedom to find you if they want.

I could let you fall on me forever
Till it's all we know.

'OK, I think I have it,' I say to Nate and J, and I get up and go to the vocal booth and sing it. We listen back to the song from the top. For the first time it feels done. The feeling you get from completing a song that has taken so long to finish is unlike much else in music. All that joy, all that relief.

Post finished song there's an exhilarated exhaustion that comes and I allow my bones back to the couch and it's not long before I am letting it drift me on its string again. This time further.

The string attaches to a yoyo and spins me into the early 90s to the beginning of heartbreak.

I'm in that same phone booth outside Lavery's on Bradbury Place making that same call. I'm 17 so I shouldn't have even been in the Manhattan nightclub but then none of us should have been. You had broken up with me about 20 minutes earlier and my heart was doing unfamiliar things. Felt like it was made of something different, had something inside it that may well have always been there but I hadn't noticed before this moment. There was perhaps a glass part of it that was now in bits, so there were shards just sloshing around in there. We don't know what heartbreak is until it happens and we don't know what the heart can take until it happens again. And again. And it feels like the hardest pain to bear, until the next time. But this was the first time so it was all I imagined the heart could take. Ooft, both my imagination and my heart were in for some surprises in the years to come.

Right this minute all I wanted was to be home. As fast as possible. Ideally beamed, like in *Star Trek*. But trying to get a taxi in Belfast in those days was like panning for gold after the gold rush had long ended. Sure, there might be a nugget in this river somewhere but you're more than likely wasting your time, son. So I called my folks. 'Can you come pick me up please?', I slurred through the umpteen 50 pence shots I had worked my way through. 'For god's sake Gary it's after midnight.' I tell my dad I just got dropped. The line goes quiet long enough for me to think we got cut off but just before I speak, he says, 'Oh Gary I'm sorry.' His son's wee heart is broken for the first time and he feels it too, I can sense it even down the phone line. He is choked up. Is my dad crying? I saw him cry only a handful of times in his life and most of those were after the dementia had set in. His voice catching, 'Here, talk to your mum.' It was, unbeknownst to me, a preview of his catchphrase for when I went over to university in Dundee if he picked up the phone when I called home, 'Here, talk to your mum.' But in this moment, it seems I'm to talk to mum because he can't find an uncracked voice.

I was, even at 17, beginning to learn that the best way to move pain from inside to outside was through creation. Making art. Making something. Making something messy is best because it mimics the pain and it attaches to it and draws it up and out like a poultice. But my dad never learned this in his lifetime, and I never knew to tell him. How do you teach your dad anything? The audacity of that thought is bewildering. It dizzies me and I stagger and the string hooks around me again and this time I'm dragged by the one foot back through to the studio couch where I appear freshly woken and being asked by Scott if I want a cuppa. 'No thanks,' I croak. 'All good.'

No one put the chasm that exists inside me. Not my first heartbreak, or my last, or any in between that I have endured or caused. I put it there myself. Or rather I built it over time, even though I think I thought I was building something else, the different parts of me perhaps uninformed of what each was building. Like some secret project that requires strict confidentially, and only when all the disparate pieces come together do you realise, too late, that you have, in fact, built a weapon.

No one else is to blame for any of this. Only me. I built the chasm inside, so it's only logical that one would eventually manifest outwardly too, pushing everyone I loved further and further away.

JACK

Part Three

24 December 2019

The uncut winter grass bends easy, flattening to the will of the rolling wind which, as if it reads my mind, roars up to let me know that I too am barely more than grass to be flattened. It climbs in under my one good coat and pinches me upright. Such insistence from Boreas, the god of the north wind. He is reminding me that this is not a dream. You are very much awake, lad. This is really happening. My finger and thumb attend to my collar, endeavouring to keep him at bay but he finds multiple new ways inside my coat, and I only have the two hands. I stop short of cursing him, figuring offending the gods today would be a mistake. Today I will bow to all the gods. I shall honour them with sycophantic compliments. Your whip still cuts deep, O mighty god of wind! And sure, I promise myself, I can get back to offending the gods tomorrow, there will always be plenty of time for that. Today though, I'll give them their due, their offerings, their deference … their sacrifices.

Tomorrow is Christmas Day, but we will have to spend its eve perched on the edge of something else. Right now I'm standing in the garden with the sea ahead of me, the forest to my left, the house behind me, and so, by the process of elimination, with only the starboard side unaccounted for, over there must be where all the oblivion is.

My mum, sister and niece have arrived outside. We are all in harmony, dressed up nice for death. What was said in the car ride to the funeral is lost to me now, but I know it wasn't morbid, or sad. Sadness for sure is drenched over everything these last few days but that doesn't mean that every moment spent in sadness is sad. Just like every moment spent in happiness is not happy. There are undulations to all the phases of life, and all the phases of death. You are never only one thing. As Johnny says to me, 27 months from today, when we first get together to start writing an album that will eventually be called *The Forest Is the Path*, no one thing can be everything and everything can't be one thing. So we drive through the sadness in our Sunday best feeling sad and happy and angry and lonely and together and brave and terrified – and all things and no things.

On our way, it being the season an' all, the houses are also dressed up. But they, unlike us, far from the gloom of funeral garb, are unapologetically cheerful in their Christmas jumpers. Flashing lights hanging off eaves and gables and brightly coloured Santas and reindeer and snowmen vie for our attentions as we pass. Some people, it's maybe unfestive to say, have gone mental, let's be honest. They have, with some gusto, thrown Christmas hard at their homes and gardens. In those dwellings it kinda looks like Santa crashed his sleigh in their front garden and they have him held hostage. 'Don't move a fucking muscle, old man, or Rudolph gets it.' But this Yuletide over-egging doesn't bother me that much, as most of me is occupied with something other than Christmas. And then it creeps in. That thought that this time of year might be changed for us from now on, and is perhaps Christmas altered now forever? But whatever that means and if it means anything at all, the question dissolves in the acid of my thoughts as quickly as it arrives. My gaze wanders above the festooned homes into the slate grey of the morning, the sky one piece of drab cloth as far as my exhausted eyes can see, as unremarkable and monochrome as it is forgetful and forgiving. You could whisper into it every single thing you regret and it would never tell a soul. I tell it I was not a good son. I tell it I was never around. I tell it I fought with him too much and for too long. And I tell it I only stopped fighting with him too late in life to make up for much of anything. I tell it. I tell it. It forgives me but I don't feel forgiven. It forgets me but I don't want to be forgotten.

As his friends and our friends and his family walk through the door of the funeral home the four of us greet them all and try our best to hold their emotions in our heavy hands as gently as we can. For them, and for us. He has such great friends. We too have such great friends. And such extraordinary family. The gathered are an exquisite bunch alright. Kind and thoughtful and some travelled from distance too. For them too small the condolence card, which genuinely would have been enough. No, they are here to stand with us, and to stand with him, for him and by him.

God, I have been racking my brain but that day blurs in me like ink in water. Did we bury him first or was it the funeral home first? The latter would make more sense of course but I think it was just family at the graveside, so I may have all this in the wrong order. You can choose for yourself which happened first. Do we bury him first, or do we talk about him first? You have 30 seconds while the board revolves to make your decision. Perhaps the studio audience will help you out. As I write all this the ink is still smudged in the corners of it. You can never really get that ink out. Of the water, or the wildlife or the beach, or the funeral where the tanker ran aground. The oily, inky atoms of it will hide in there for all time.

This will be a humanist service. The irony is not lost on us as when my sister and I were younger he insisted we go to church. He though, did not go. But he insisted, so we went. So it was down to my mum to drag us out the door of a Sunday and haul us off to our moral education. I laugh to myself in the door of the funeral home thinking not even at the end, not even *after* the end, old man, did you deign to set foot in a church. You always got your way.

Seats are taken and the celebrant makes a start on the beginning of the end. I am suddenly standing reading a eulogy I wrote last night at about 4 a.m. I don't remember walking up here to the lectern to read it. I don't remember starting to read it. I just remember it being read. Or it reading me.

Does everything ending take a piece of you with it?

My voice catches at one point talking about how much her grandfather loved my niece, and it's as if there might be tears after all but I take a few deep breaths and they never materialise. But I am clearly flagging a bit so my sister, bless her, leaves her seat and takes up a position right beside me as if to say to those gathered, 'If you're gonna fight him you'll have to fight me an' all.' I'm always proud to be her brother, well since we stopped fighting with each other anyway, but in that moment, I have never been prouder to call her my sister.

I hear later that day that someone opened a plastic-wrapped boiled sweet during my eulogy and it was the loudest thing ever, the whole place listening to the crackling cacophony with stifled laughter. When I hear this, it makes me happy. I like all the things today that my dad would have laughed at. Either that or he would have lost his temper, roaring 'Will yous for god's sake stop it with the sweetie wrappers.' Either way it would have been funny. So I'm good with it.

I didn't hear the plastic being unwrapped. In my memory I still don't hear it. File not found. Drowned out maybe by the crunch and hissing and the collapsing and grinding of the fall of the only empire I've ever known. The fabled founder of the Roman empire, Romulus, and the last Roman emperor, Romulus Augustulus, shared the same name. So on a day like today, as at many points through history, there feels a cyclical futility and inevitability in all things. We can rise and fall the same as we ever were, with nothing much changing in between. If you believe in an afterlife, I'm envious of you. I have wanted so much, and for so long, to believe in one. Some days the only way to make sense of the world is that there is no sense to be made of it, and that therefore this cannot be all of it. There must be more. More afterwards. The end is not the end. I want desperately to believe that, today of all days. That he'll go on. That he'll find some peace and the fog of the last near decade will lift and he will rise up and out into his old self again. Into the best version of himself. He'll see his father and his mother again and they will all know what it feels like to be reunited, and we will follow after and know the same. But you see, the thing is, I don't know. So instead I try to count the things I do know. My father is dead. One. End of list.

My sister, uncles, cousins and myself are at the back of the hearse, getting instructions on how to lift the coffin. I'm not really listening. Much like when someone on the other end of the phone is reading back a food order I've just made. Try as I might to listen to them my ears go offline until they finish talking and then I say, 'That all sounds right,' though having no clue if it is. Maybe nobody else in this huddle around the coffin is listening either, but when the fella asks if we understand we all say yes. What I think I understand is that I am about to help carry a box that contains my dad over to a hole in the ground that we're going to lower him into, cover with him dirt, and then leave him there. Is that about right? OK, then I understand. The gents lift the coffin and lower it over the six of us. The edge bites down hard on my right shoulder. It is the last time you'll touch me. Your hand on my shoulder. We walk following each other as much as we are following no one. The weight is biblical. Feels like this weight is not measured in stones and pounds, but in centuries. Honestly, how aren't more of these dropped? I shudder to think of it. The worst day of someone's life made far worse still. The thought of dropping him runs through me like a poison and I put a call out to all my atoms to be as careful in this moment as they have ever been. We shuffle past the reminders of those that have already made this slow, short, endless journey. Gravestones giving the briefest summations of lives lived. As if your name, the day you are born and the day you die are all you are.

As the coffin is lowered into the freshly carved-out grave I notice not too far away, in fact way too close, are the two men that dug this hole. It's a jarring sight. A little bit like seeing the stagehands of a play lurking in the wings waiting for the next scene change, doing nothing wrong at all, nothing other than being professional, poised and ready to spring into action when the actors leave the stage and the lights are dimmed, but also making you far too aware that everything you're witnessing is a charade. If an actor that communicates with the audience is breaking the fourth wall, are these two men breaking the fifth? Some extra wall that we should never see past, as to see beyond it makes life far too real for anyone to be able to handle, or comprehend. Like the unmasking of the not so great and powerful Oz. Or Charlton Heston pounding his fists into the sand after a shuddering realisation. Or the trusted narrator of a story finally revealed, all this time, to be the villain. One of the men is leaning on the grip handle of his shovel in a way that feels too casual for the occasion. I think to myself, 'Give the guy a break, he's probably knackered from digging this big fucking hole.' But his shovel blade has fresh dark mud clung to it and when I look around for any other new holes and find none but the one we're standing over, my stomach turns as if the fresh dark mud on the blade is in fact fresh dark blood. That mud was once where my father is now being lowered. The fifth wall has been broken. Smashed to bits. This is too real now. Heaney, trying to rescue me perhaps, returns to my thoughts in this moment. That same poem in that same Coleraine accent.

'. . . a clean rasping sound
When the blade sinks into gravelly ground:

My father, digging. I look down.'

My father . . . dug.

There are two bands of strong fabric looped under the coffin and four men, two on either side, have a hand gripping each of the ends. Those ribbons are taut and rigid against the weight of you, a weight not long from our shoulders, and have you held in midair. Six foot under, that's what they say. 'Oh Stevie, he's six foot under, poor Stevie.' Maybe someone will say that of you some day. Today maybe. Oh Jack, he's six foot under, poor Jack. They lower you down slowly. Slower than anything I have ever known. It could be six foot, it could be six miles. I feel caught between wanting this to be over and never wanting this to end. Pulled by horses between those two thoughts, my skin pulled tight, fascia ripping, bones dislocating. With the fabric bands falling slack the coffin finds its place and the ribbons are pulled up fast, as if running for their lives lest they be buried too, their whipped-through caress being the last thing that touches you. Pulled away like you were contagious. And now that everything and anything that was down there with you, bar the mud, has deserted you I have never felt more alive, but not by levity or lightness of spirit, no, only by comparison.

I hear your snoring coming up from the hole you've just been placed into for safe keeping. It rattles the walls of your coffin like it used to rattle the walls of our house. I would hear it in my room at night and always wondered how the hell our mum ever slept. Like, ever. It's 35 years ago and I hear you loud in your sleep through that same bedroom wall, me in my room trying to find my own sleep. I'm nine years old and in the preliminary moments of what will be the first serious fever of my short life to that point, and it will bend time and space around me like a jujitsu choke hold.

Forty-eight hours previous you had said, 'Let's have a movie night.' You'd heard about a good one that's on TV tonight. This was back when TV was just the four channels and when a VHS tape cost about a week's wages, so the only chance of seeing a decent movie in our house was the rare occurrence of a rental from the local video store or watching a movie on the telly that had already been out for about ten years. The second option was free. So, ten-year-old blockbuster on the telly it was then! But I was thrilled just to be hanging out with you so it didn't matter. A movie for grown-ups with my da! A da who didn't watch a lot of movies and who clearly hadn't read the summary of the one we were about to watch. As I said, I'm nine years old.

The film starts. There's a woman swimming in the ocean in the middle of the night lit by a big American moon. Fine so far. Then a tug of cello, quiet at first. Then more insistent. Then picking up pace. My heart begins to race, not sure why yet but I am already sure this isn't gonna work out well for her. The woman who had been splashing around happily to that point then jolts suddenly. Then jolts again. Then starts thrashing about wildly crying out in pain. My memory falters here because my hands come up over my eyes. I watch the rest of the movie like this. My heart, in sympathy with the poor woman perhaps, feels like it is thrashing about in the water of me, beating in my brain one second and my feet the next. I think to myself, 'Why would anyone watch this for fun?'

Back to two nights later, that shark had haunted my dreams in the previous night's sleep so I was reluctant to close my eyes. I find myself beginning to circle the drain of what I didn't know yet was a high fever and cry out to my mum, past the Olympic level snoring of my sleeping father. If he wasn't quite Olympic level he got very close to it in the regional trials. I'm trying to work out how he can sleep after seeing the same movie I saw. The door opens and mum does the hand on forehead test and proclaims a temperature and I fall precipitously into it now that confirmation has been made of my condition, as if the fever somehow needed a permission slip from my mother to fully take hold. 'Yes, you have a fever,' she says, the fever then puts out a call to all the bacteria in the vicinity, 'OK lads, get him!' After all, the only way a vampire can gain entry to your home is if you invite them in.

I can see from here, aged 43, all the strata of my life. The slices of sedimentary rock telling the geological story of my years from now at your graveside to then watching *Jaws* through the cracks in my wee fingers. That shark swims in every layer. In every piece of me that shark patrols the waters, the levels, the degrees. 'You'll never go back in the water again', one of the taglines of the movie promises. It would take me decades to chew my way out of that divination. And the home that I have now found in the water, the healing, magical, mending, profound place that it is to me now, will be obscured from me for all those years by the heavy curtain of my fear. A fear that was fired in the kiln of this delirium, and has now taken full control of me.

In the next week or so my mum tries in vain to get me to drink some water. She lifts my head towards the glass in her other hand but every one of her efforts is batted away with all my feeble might. 'Jaws is in the glass,' I will shout out. I will fall into brief flickers of sleep only to immediately roar awake swimming away from the endless teeth of a great shark seconds from devouring me. In and out I fall of its mouth like a doomed Quint, repeating and repeating. Strange to be so removed from reality by a 100 plus temperature and yet be so profoundly changed by what you find there, in the untethered. That fever built a shark inside me, threw life into it, and left it there, hunting. Some Trojan horse, decorated to look like a gift, but containing all the ingredients of my fallibility. That shark in me, fashioned from every scrap of fear that I will ever know, will eat me from the inside out. 'It's just a film' I would hear my mum say in the rare times when my condition allowed my ears to listen. 'It's just a film. Jaws is not in the water. It is not in the glass. It is not in the bath.' But it was. It is. Even now, 40 years later, that shark, assembled in me then, is always in me, and the shark is always in the water. The trick I have found to life though, and the trick to fear, but which took me so long to figure out, is you have to get in the damn water anyway. And you will find there, in the water, a way to love the shark. And when you love the shark, you'll find a way to love yourself. Maybe. I'm told these things take time.

The fever and your snoring ebb away and there is stillness now descended over your new habitat. Our heads bowed over your grave but perhaps, like me, not in prayer. I am thinking about the earth. Soon to be everywhere you look in any direction. Everything you see. I can't leave you in there with all that dirt, so I pull you out of there in my mind.

What exactly dies when we die? And what is left behind? Just the body, or does something else remain? Is it entirely incumbent upon those of us who remember you to keep you alive or do you leave something behind for us? Something like a soul. Or a ghost. Or a consciousness.

Ask ten philosophers what consciousness is and you'll get ten different answers. Same outcome if you ask ten neuro-scientists. It is the one thing we share and the first thing we disagree on. Perhaps it is in fact the source of all the dis-agreements we have on planet Earth. If we can't agree on what sparked the life into us, or what that spark even is, or from its vantage point how we see the world, how can we agree on anything else? And whatever it is, does it die when we die? What I think about it all is immaterial but I'll say it anyway … while reality is the sea we *all* swim in (whether we want to or not), consciousness is the sea you swim in alone. A sea poured only for you. The liquid truth of your individual life. No one else can swim in your sea of perception. And you can't swim in anyone else's. There is no *Being John Malkovich* machine where we can see the world from the perspective of someone else. There is no door into anyone else's consciousness. Just the wide open space of your own. A curse if you let it curse you, a privilege if you want it.

I once read that consciousness is a painting the mind makes of itself. That our consciousness grows and evolves with every glint of light that finds its way into our eyes and neurons and brain. This happens whether we like it, or effort it, or not. This happens in spite of ourselves. Our consciousness is continually painting a vast canvas that expands ever further, creating a universe inside us that will never be completed.

But it will one day fall. Fall inwards, downwards, like yours did.

Entropy is a constant in nature. Order will eventually fall to disorder. The active mind will one day crumble to ruin. But did your dementia take *everything* with it? Did it leave you with nothing to share with us in the afterworld? Nothing at all?!

Or are there strands of your life still lingered? Little hairs of light curled around the ending of you that unfurled when your body lay at rest and that float around us now in the ether, infinite. Deathless. Follicles of your essence that will live with us always. I would love to think this is true. That we all leave something behind us in our wake. A ripple of us eternal. When I think of it, I see it. OK then, maybe it is the thought itself that conjures it. So perhaps that's further proof that our afterlives only exist in the minds of those that continue. This is the insidious whirlpool of the ultimate unanswerable question: what happens when we die? The endless possibilities loop and twist around each other like so many question marks writhing.

Maybe all that happens when we end is that we are not audible. Maybe when these conversations and arguments rage, about death and lives and afterlives, we are indeed joining in the discussion but we can no longer be heard by the living. Maybe there are pieces of you, strands of you, shouting at me now while I write this: 'I am here, I am right here, can you not see me! This! This is where you go when you die ... Here. Right here. Beside you. Now.'

ALBUM THEME 4

Death

February 2024

I'm always dressed wrong for London. Too many layers or, more often, not enough. Today, aside from this last 15 minutes, it's the latter. I take my seat on the train I barely made, highlighted, a little too passive–aggressively in my opinion, by it pushing off from the station just as my arse lands on the seat. Perhaps I pressed the accelerator with my backside. I've an odd winter sweat on me from running for the train. Face near frozen off, back dripping wet. One of those winter sprints after which you can feel all the teeth in your head without using your tongue. This train, I hope, assuming in my haste I didn't get on the wrong one, is pointed in the general direction of the studio. We are nearly done recording. Normally I would be happy to be coming to the end as it means a tour is not far away and we get to go play live, but this time I have felt a hint of sadness hanging off me, albeit gently, swinging ever so slightly from the thinnest of my threads. I think I figured out what it was this morning. I've really loved these last few weeks and I don't want them to end. I'll talk to J and Nate about it later and they'll say they were thinking the same exact thing. Who ever said sadness couldn't make you happy?

I burrow into my seat and try and get as comfortable as one can while itching with sweat and hurriedness. The headphones go on. I listen to a series of talks, the first of which is about the Fire Sermon by the Buddha. The world is on fire, says the Buddha to his monks, the eye is burning, the nose is burning, the body is burning, the mind is burning. OK, this isn't as calm as I was hoping for, and surely we need that fire inside sometimes, but I understand, as I have felt these destructive fires inside me and I know the damage they have wrought. The train, only away from the station ten minutes, grinds to a halt and I internally groan and get immediately frustrated. Then I catch myself and laugh inwardly at the fact that even while listening to a talk about Buddhism I can still get instantly irritated by tiny inconveniences.

But as trivial as this slight stall in the journey is, it touches ever so slightly into the lake of fire that resides in me. Every argument, every word in anger I have ever said hisses and bubbles in that lake still. That lake remembers everything. But also what of the good the fire in me has done? Yes, anger and resentment and hate and fear have risen from that fire but surely, at least in part, passion and art and creativity and adventure are born there too. So every song we have ever written, every gig we have ever played, every journey into the unknown we have ever set out on is also lit by fire. So are there two fires in us all? Or just one, that can both warm our hearths and burn us to cinder? I tune back into the talk again and the Buddha says it is suffering that causes these fires to burn through us and our desire causes suffering. The end of suffering can be sought though, by letting go of our anger, greed, resentment and ill will, and that end of suffering is called nirvana.

The train coughs forward a little and then lurches but not onwards towards the terminus, instead backwards. I let out a, this time, audible groan of frustration at the reversal of direction of travel, but then realise something is different. We are moving in silence and the carriage, which before was peppered with a handful of fellow passengers, has suddenly emptied out. Just me and my frustration taking a backwards train ride together. We gather pace and make no undulations or turns. It is a straight route now to wherever we are going so impossibly backwards, and soon enough I find the destination is 1991, just in time to get the bus home from school.

On I get and sit down beside my friend Mark. He had left the school grounds at lunch to go get the new Nirvana album on cassette tape and had managed, good effort by the way, to listen to the first half of the album during the afternoon classes, and now side two is ready to play. He offers his headphones for me to take hold of one side. In those days you took one side, your pal the other, and you had to twist the headphones round and hold the orange-foam-covered pad to your ear, all the while with the tight metal frame pulling against your grip, trying to spring back into its preferred semi-circular shape. Not sure what metal those frames were built of then but god they were durable, almost unbreakable as I recall. Once released they would spring back into place again as if nothing had been twisted. Oh, to be fashioned of that material. Mark presses play. What happens next only went in the one ear but roared through my whole body like lightning and prophesy.

'Come on people now, smile on your brother, everybody get together, try to love one another right now.' Then a handful of menacing tugs of guitar turning quickly to frenzy and somewhere in there the line 'gotta find a way, a better way'. Yip, a better way, I think I just found it. Or it found me. I can't tell yet, but something just happened. The sound is only in my left ear, so this could be a stroke. But even though it's only being poured into one ear, it fills all of me with fire.

The two most important, formative, moments of my life happened in that year. First, in English class, hearing Heaney's words for the first time, and now on the bus barely two minutes away from school having my future screamed into me one ear at a time. The first formative moment felt like a call to finally listen, this one, this second moment feels like a call to arms. Every stop on that backwards train ride through my life leads unshakeably to this moment now. My whole life changed without me knowing it right this minute. But this version of me that has lived his whole life, the version on the backwards train ride, knows where it all leads. This 15-year-old version only knows one thing, all the world is on fire, his ears are on fire, his eyes are on fire, his soul is on fire.

The English train shunts forwards and all the carriages obey, grudgingly at first, and we're off again. The map to the end of suffering plays on my headphones still and I tune in again and then out again like too many switches clicking on and off. The journey winds through London and gives brief glimpses into lives lived on streets I'll probably never walk down. The train slows but doesn't stop this time next to a five-a-side football match seeming to say, 'Here, you like football, watch this'. There is a clear offside as a goal hanger scores an inglorious tap-in and runs off celebrating like he's just won the Champions League with the last kick of the game. Fuck's sake mate! I realise I say this out loud and look around to see if any of the other passengers heard me. No it seems. Or they don't care. Or they just hope beyond hope that I'm not some nutjob trying to, oh horror of all horrors, start a conversation with them. I think about how much I crave connection and at the same time am so terrified at the thought of anyone actually trying to talk to me. Are we all caught in that? Begging for someone to understand us but so goddamn scared that, if given the chance, people would run from us if they heard what we had to say, like we're

Frankenstein's homework. I think about the person across from me being able to hear my thoughts and I panic. I try to stop thinking. And of course it has the opposite effect and revs the engine of my thought so loud that I'm now certain all thoughts are escaping my ears like steam, like when that officious EPA agent in *Ghostbusters* makes them shut down the storage facility and all the phantoms are freed and they fly out and wreak havoc on New York. My thoughts burst and fly and climb and lumber out of my mind and smash down over London, bringing it to its knees. 'Sorry London,' I whisper so quiet no one can hear, as the train drags me off outta there like a getaway driver.

The outside is switched off by a tunnel and the dark of it is lit through the window on my left shoulder in bursts of lamplight that phase and voom like strobe and it becomes as if there's a swinging pocket watch in front of me and I drift and lull to its visual beating and, gradually at first, then rising seismically upwards, I start to hear the music from that incredible night. It gets louder and louder until it's pristine in my 16-year-old ears. Ears ready to begin their dismantling. And I open my eyes in 1992 in the middle of a flailing mosh pit in the King's Hall, Belfast towards the end of Nirvana's one and only show in the city. The last song of which is the first song I heard on that school bus ride. 'I gotta find a way, a better way' Kurt screams into the microphone like some manic pilot of a plane I don't know I've boarded. The start is the end and the end is the start.

For us that have gathered, we are in communion, synchronisation, concert. Funny how we use that word now, concert. Like it always meant gig, or show. But it means togetherness. Symbiosis. Agreement. Alliance. Tonight is an alliance of souls, of spirits. In fact not spirits at all, spirit, singular. Oneness.

In this room tonight it feels like there is a map being drawn in fire. Or perhaps Nirvana drew the map already and they are just singing it out to us contour by contour and, if we want to, we can pick up again and feel it aflame in our hands at any time hence. And I do. We all do. I know people that were there that night, all of whom were profoundly changed. Signal fires lit then, still blazing now.

A couple of years from tonight Noel Gallagher would write and his brother Liam would sing the line 'don't put your life in the hands of a rock 'n' roll band', but Christ, on a night like tonight I can't think of anything I'd rather do.

We didn't have many international artists playing shows in Northern Ireland at the time. Most bands were too afraid to play here. But any artist that came to Belfast in those days we worshiped from then on. The year before Red Hot Chili Peppers played the Ulster Hall and we all went and they were golden for us forever. The Chilis will always be tattooed on my heart from that night. And Nirvana, well there is a case to be made for that band and that night to be when my heart started beating properly for the first time. That they were in fact my first love.

Later that night as I lay in my bed, the gig still ringing in my ears like a long echo, I feel that new heart beating like a kick drum, Dave Grohl's right foot still thumping out an encore that I had somehow carried home with me. I didn't want it to ever end. The following day when I wake up to no ringing in my ears I feel a genuine sadness, like that morning was the end of the gig and not 'Territorial Pissings'. I look at my mum and my sister and my dad at the breakfast table and I feel like I have been given some secret knowledge and I want to tell them all what I have discovered but don't, because I realise, then it wouldn't be a secret.

And without any warning the train leaves the tunnel with a sucking pop and, ta-da, London has vanished revealing countryside thrown out liberally beside me left and right, and in the green of it there is less to think about, and it seems to want to promise me simplicity. I take the hint and I decide to practise letting go. Can't do it. Well, I gave it a good try. OK, OK I'll try harder.

What of the fire that was lit back then, 30-some years ago, at that gig? I can feel it burning still. Did it lead me all the way here? Did that fire light the touchpaper on every song I ever wrote? And what of the other fire that burns through me? My anger, my resentment, my jealousy, my delusion. I want to believe they are two distinct fires. One that drives us forward, the engine of our artistry, our soul, our romance, our divinity, our ecstasy. The other that holds us back, or even worse tries to burn us and everyone we love to ash. Can you douse one fire and keep the other, or do they both go out?

I think about all the stupid things I have said in anger. I want to corral them all in a vast lasso and drag them back to me and stamp them as unsaid. Unbrand them. Hearing the backwards fizz of a branding in reverse. ZZIF. Upon the cue of that sound each one gets taken back because it was never said. Every friend I have lost is returned. The angry metal of any resentment forged turns to quicksilver and scurries away in a glistening river, and in its wake, harmony is restored.

Outside the window of the train the English countryside is spotlit through the clouds in fanning beams of sunlight and I see a festival crowd out in the endless fields. We are on stage at V Festival 2007. We're told that we are co-headliners with Foo Fighters. Ha. Let me let you into a wee secret, there is no such thing as co-headliners. Anyone ever tells you they are co-headlining a festival ask them if they're on last. If they're not they ain't headlining. No shame in being second on the bill, especially to the mighty Foos, but we're not kidding ourselves that we are sharing the top of the bill with them. They are on last, and therefore headlining. As it should be. So here we are right in the middle of our not-headlining set and 'Chasing Cars' is the next song on the list. Before we play it, I take a moment to tell the audience a story. I'll do that. Blather on in between songs, I mean. Most of the time it's some off-the-cuff nonsense that falls out of my mouth unfiltered but this is from a deep place in my heart. I talk

119

about what it means to be playing on the same stage as the Foos and that their frontman, Mr Grohl, was in the band that changed my life and made sense of everything and is the reason why I'm standing here today, and that I want to dedicate this next song to Nirvana for all they did for me. In the middle of me saying all that a great cheer from the crowd rose up mid-sentence and, as the timing was a bit off, I was confused for a second, until that is I looked to my left and saw to my amazement Dave Grohl walking out towards me at the microphone with the biggest smile on his face. He put his arms around me and said 'Thanks, man' and we stood there a second, him and I, and in that second a universe came and went. The slowness of time, a second lasting forever, I saw my 16-year-old self, standing stock still in the throb of the mosh staring up at me through time to some 15 years later wondering how the fuck this grown-up version of me got to here. 'How the hell did this happen?' he asks me as he reaches up through time to share this moment with me. When that wormhole closes, I watch Dave walk away and off the stage. All I could muster to say into the mic was, 'Well that doesn't happen every day.' Yes, I could've said something better, believe me I wanted to, but gimme a break as I wasn't even sure what way was up. Or perhaps my 16-year-old self had remained and I had fallen through time to live my life over again. I just hope that I'm better the next time round.

In my headphones I hear that anger is like picking up a hot coal and expecting it to burn someone else. I don't want to pick up those stones anymore. I don't want them. There is a good death in the end of anger, in the end of resentment, in the end of jealousy. Dying so one can live is the best kind of death. All those things made in that fire serve us not one bit. But sometimes in my life I have felt holding onto that fire feels like the only way to stay alive. I know now I was just plain wrong. But it took me way too long to figure that out.

So then, what fires need to stay lit for heat and food and passion and art and creativity and what fires need to be extinguished, the fires that ignite jealousy, rage, resentment, anger, delusion? Can I kill one and not the other? Can I find a way to a good death so I can live?

There is a synchronicity, a reverberation, that can only be felt if you're listening for it. There's an energy in the universe that is trying to tell you everything. All the times you trip and fall that energy just told you to watch where you're going. We just don't hear it. Every time we hurt someone with our words or actions the universe is telling us to be kind. We just don't hear it. But if I check my ego and I breathe slow and listen carefully I can sometimes hear it telling me everything I need to know. If I check my ego. My ego. Something else that needs to die.

While the train finds more of England to roll through, I close my eyes and think of all the fires that I have lit and the few I have put out. The ones I'm glad for and the ones I'm ashamed of. All these fires rise now in my mind until there is nothing else but flames. I cannot tell which fire is which, or if there are even two fires at work here, or has it always been one? But I know for sure I am done with the anger, the delusion, the jealousy and the resentment. I just don't want them anymore. Whatever this fire is meant for I no longer want it for anything but music and love and art and creativity. In the end I guess it's about discernment. When I feel a song rising in me, I pick up my guitar. So when I feel anger rising, maybe I just do the opposite and I don't pick it up. I am still though, and always will be, a work in progress.

ALBUM THEME 5

Life

March 2024

'I'm not afraid to wander endlessly
I just don't know how to be found'

From 'The Forest Is the Path'

Home in Bangor and, from my window, night begins to impose itself on the garden. The street lamps show me the makings of a storm about to teach all the trees a lesson. They are beginning to bend to its will, shivering first, but not long till they are genuflecting. The crows have deserted them but this is nothing new as they always do, the fickle creatures evacuating before the dark makes its landfall. The promise of night had already hurried them before the storm got the chance to. Such a strange ritual they perform every day and

I feel privileged to witness it when I do. Dusk begins and the crows circle the trees, then jostle for prime spots, some fighting hard for their berth, then a stillness descends as if they are all settling in for sleep, but just before the last layer of blue is pulled away from the sky to reveal the night, they all explode out like fireworks made of soot, and race to nestle in the rooftops instead. Every single night they do this. Thirty crepuscular minutes in the trees, but they'll be in the rooftops before dark. I haven't been able to figure out the logic of it but I know they, as do all animals, have a secret knowledge we aren't privy to and therefore there must be some reason for it, even if that reason is incomprehensible to the likes of me. Every evening, they take their transitional, momentary perch before rising like phoenixes to assume their preferred sleeping quarters. And on the evenings I see it, I feel like I am being shown something deep and elemental, as if I have been given a map to something unnamed but important with no landmarks and no clue what lies where X marks the spot.

The dance of crows is a strange music that heavies my eyes and staggers me a little, but I hold fast because I want their secret knowledge. I want any knowledge. Some. A slice. A portion. A morsel. Beyond the garden is a forest, out there in front of me, waiting inside the storm, a signal I only hear on nights like this, when everything is trying its utmost to drown that signal out. I feel like I might know why, and I am antsy to walk out to it. To get out into it. It hungers me towards it. As if offering something to me, and only in the offering do I know that it's what I want. And though the forest is calling me out beyond the galloping storm, the tempest bids me hold. 'Stay there,' it says, 'if you know what's good for you.' The forest a beckoner. The storm a reckoning. Or is it the other way around?

I have a habit of ignoring good advice though, so I walk out into it. The storm first. Swimming through the dark. Trying to get to something. Get at something. There is a path here, I can feel it. A path only visible when all you can see is nothing. There is a path that opens to you when night descends. There is a path when there is no path at all. Almost all the light is gone now, save for the flickering pulse of the lighthouse across the bay which falls achingly close, but doesn't quite stretch far enough, to break the dark seal of the forest ahead of me. If anything it seems to say, 'Here is a place not to go. Here is a land you are not supposed to know about. Here is everything you cannot have.'

The forest paying no mind to the storm, calls out again under the clamour of the wind. 'Everything you ever wanted to know is in here,' it sings.

The rain is thrown sideways by the storm into my hood and it slashes at my eyes like bayonets. It seems everything but the forest itself will try to keep me from it. From here I can see the edge of it and beyond it looks to be where all light goes to die. A black hole that feeds on all our fear. All our inadequacies. All our guilt. All our regret. The wind whispers to me a warning, it tells me that in there snap the great fanged mouths of all the wolves and sharks that ever hunted you. They swim in the belly of the forest. In there is everything you have ever done to hurt someone, every single word of it. In there is your father, and if you find him to ask for his forgiveness, he will never offer it to you. That is if he even remembers you. His mind is separated from his body in there. They wander apart from each other. Cursed to be wraiths and to be strangers. He will not know you. You will barely know him. Your heart will be ripped out of your chest and you will watch it beat its last, right in front of your eyes. There is no time in there, but when you return, if you return, if you can find your way back out again, everything out here will have aged hundreds of years. Everyone you know will be dead. And so all the answers you seek, even if you were to find them in there, will be rendered meaningless.

But still I walk on towards the forest.

One foot follows the other as if by the pull of some force I can't name: Destiny, perhaps? Belligerence, more likely. I am mere yards from its border. Stopped now but the tug of it is on me. The knotted trees reach out to me, and all the while behind me the wind screams its warnings into my ears. 'This is your last chance. You will not come back from this. I cannot protect you in there. This will be the end of you and everything you have ever known.'

So, do I believe the forest, or do I believe the storm?

I decide I believe the forest.

This is not a door but I walk through anyway. There is no path. There is no light. There are no signs to show me the way. There are no answers. And almost immediately I make my peace with that, and it feels like the first thing I truly know. So I no longer know nothing. And that feels like the first step to something.

My fear is in here. My guilt. My panic. My father too. Sharks swim around me, and eels, and the shining eyes of wolves dot the edges of my visual field. But, somehow, I feel no danger, no jeopardy. All these things of me seem to be floating, not fixed. They do not attack. I begin to get the feeling they are actually guarding me. There is no path, only forest. My father takes my hand and says, 'Wake up, son, you have so much further you need to go.'

Outside the forest the storm continues, and the pummelling rain too. The faint swinging beam of the lighthouse drags across the dark, seemingly impenetrable border of the forest and, in each rotation, there is the briefest of spotlights on the place where I once stood waiting to believe the forest. But I am no longer there.

JACK

Part Four

December 2020

It's near year's end, the ninth month of lockdown coiled like a pit of snakes around the world. It is close to a year since the old man died and I'm burrowed into Los Angeles like a tick.

When this new era began, I felt, even if I had known how to grieve, I couldn't bring my grief in with me anyway. That would be too self-pitying, surely. No place to feel sorry for oneself when we collectively have bigger shit to deal with and I thought any of my prior pain should be left behind. Perhaps there was a bouncer on the door of these times holding up a hand and, with the weary air of someone who'd seen it all before, saying, 'You can come in fella, but your mate (gestures over my shoulder to my nascent grief) ... look at the state of him, he's hammered.' Behind me my grief, shakily maintaining verticality just about and blinking slowly, trying with all his might to stay cool, to stay upright, mutters, 'I'm fine, mate, I'm fine.' But he wasn't fooling anyone. So I left him there swaying behind me and walked alone through the door of this new era. He'll find his own way, I thought to myself. And he did. Eventually. It took him the bones of a year though.

And as the door closed behind him, I heard him utter one baleful word of longing and confusion, 'but …'

Over this last year I have sat down at my desk so many times to write something about you. Failing, I fail every time, I instead try to write something about anything. I make shapes that look an awful lot like words sometimes but they mean nothing at all. Less than nothing. They are forced onto the page and then become prisoners of it. Captives holding today's newspaper up to the camera telling the world in hoarse monosyllables they are being treated well, but their cuts, bruises and emaciation tell a different story. I can command these words what to do, but I can't make them mean it. I've pushed them too hard and squeezed them too tight. Tried to get the toothpaste out of a tube that has been rolled flat too many times already with the back of the brush. I write a Post-it note reminding myself to buy toothpaste and go over and stick it to the door so I don't forget, only to find the note I already stuck there yesterday reminding me to get toothpaste. I cover my entire life with Post-it notes so as not to forget to live it. Buy toothpaste. Get milk. Collect mail. You need stamps. Write a song. Water plants. Avoid dealing with the existential crisis you are in the twelfth month of because when you do it's gonna hurt … like a lot. A third note with buy toothpaste written on it. Ack, shit!!!!!

Pulling the fridge door open in LA and staring at all the things I have run out of, I suddenly find myself holding our fridge open 30 years ago in Bangor. I can't hear anything yet but I see them all around the dinner table. My mum, my sister and yes there, alive in the past, is you. You look angry, but I still can't hear you. I'm home from Glasgow, and according to the decorations that adorn the house, it's Christmas. The millennium is knocking on the door. This is not the day, 20 some years in the future, that you will die on but it's not far off. I take the can of Coke I must have been in there looking for and close the fridge door. When it closes the sound clicks in … 'Pinko liberal nutjob' is how you round off your point. Ah, we're arguing about politics it seems. Our sweet spot. I dive right in. 'Right-wing maniac' I call you and we fall to it like wolves. So many arguments and fights between the two of us that my mum cried through, trying in vain to get us to stop. So much time wasted.

Between the ages of 15 and 35 my father and I would fight about everything. Literally anything could set us off. Mostly though it was about politics, sometimes (until I was 29 and Snow Patrol had our first hits) it was about me wasting my life with all this music nonsense. 'You need a proper job, son.

135

You can't keep going with this lark. You're kidding yourself.' Thinking about it now it perhaps sounds crazy given how things turned out, but you were right. I was kidding myself. There are infinite strands of the multiverse where SP never made it. Every other strand in fact, other than this one. Never had a hit. Never even one successful year, never mind 20. We had been banging our heads against a brick wall for a decade before it all happened for us. You saw that. Thinking back, it probably broke your heart to see your son humbled so many times, and just getting right back up again covered in mud for another beating. A glutton for punishment. Thing is though, I loved it. And I would do it all again the exact same way.

I'd just do it, next time round, without all the fighting with you.

You wanted me to see things your way, and I simply would not entertain it. Your way was just plain wrong I would think. I could not conceive of a world in which your way was the right way. I was pig-headed. Idealistic. Stubborn. I knew everything and you knew nothing. I am so thoroughly ashamed right down to my very molecules to think of it now. If I had any agency in this memory, I would slap my younger self hard on the face and tell him to sit down and shut the fuck up, or better still, just say something kind.

I think I know now that all you really wanted was for me to make sense to you. You did not understand me, but it was not your fault. You were born in 1938! The year before the start of the Second World War. Your teenage years were the 1950s for god's sake. The word 'teenager' had not even been invented yet. The youth, and many other, revolutions of the following decade would come too late for you. Here you are now, a time traveller from the 50s, fighting with a son that makes music that must hit your ears like thrown fistfuls of gravel.

You and your own father did everything together. When you and my mum got married your mum and dad even moved in next door! I like none of what you like at this moment in my life, as the year 2000 approaches, 61 years after your arrival on planet Earth. To you I must be rebellion incarnate. All you wanted was to recognise your son and the only way you knew how to do that was to find something of yourself in him. And I wouldn't let myself be you. The man who, as a child, I had idolised I now wanted to be the opposite of. God, I so wish in this moment, in all these moments of saying hurtful things to you I shudder to think of now, I wish I could show myself all that wasted time. All that time I would never get back. Can never get back. I carry all that with me still. I have never found a place to put it down. A place that might forgive me. There is no shelf upon which this fits. No shelf I've found that can bear the weight of it. A weight meant for me alone to lift and no one else. An Excalibur of regret forged only for me.

The Buddhist monk Ajahn Chah was reportedly a gruff man. Wise beyond words but brusque with it. Him and his followers were out for a walk one day. They happened upon a clearing up ahead of them and in it stood a massive rock. Ajahn Chah pointed up at it and said to one of his acolytes, 'That rock up there, is it heavy?' The young monk replied, 'Yes, master, very heavy.' The old monk grunted, displeased with the answer. 'It is only heavy,' he said, 'if you try to lift it.'

So do I just put this down. Is it as simple as that? Is it simple? Seems that way. Only an action. Set it down. Just let go of it. Easy, right? But clinging to this weight like moss is a paradox. A weight I cannot bear yet cannot put down, because what if I put it down and leave it behind me, and I leave my father there too? Behind me in my wake. What if this weight is all I have of you? This weight that strains between the fingertips of my outstretched arms and jams in under my chin like a stack of old books. Within the pages of these dusty tomes is everything I ever said to you, and everything you ever said to me. So every cruel word is trapped alongside every word of encouragement and care. To set the hurtful words down means I must leave the rest too. If only I could just write over every terrible thing I ever said to you in anger, replacing it with how I feel now. Scribble out every coarse word from these books that are so heavy in my arms. I take it all back. All of it. Every word said in frustration. I didn't mean it. I take all of it back! Please, let me take it back.

But you aren't here. And I never said I was sorry within the span of your life. So that sorry does not exist between the brackets of your birth and your death. And there cannot be a sorry for you, because it sits here beside me still, fully dressed, bags packed, but always waiting.

I put my head down on my kitchen table. Reminds me of school. Put your head down on your desk, Lightbody. God knows I was no bright spark in my early schooldays. Me being made to study the wood grain of my desk would certainly make it easier on the teacher than actually trying to teach me something. It would have been easier to teach the desk. The kitchen table feels heavy on my forehead. Again I have the sense that the world is on upside down. Surely gravity would dictate that I would be the heavy part of this scenario, my forehead being on top an' all. But I feel the desk pushing up at me, demanding to be in charge. Bullied by an inanimate object, surely a new low. I wear the desk for a little while until I think it's actually trying to tell me something, perhaps listing the things I need to let go of.

Putting down the weight is one thing. Putting down all the things that are upside down in one's life is something else entirely. First question, an important one, which way is down?

I have a playlist on random in the background, Frank Ocean's 'Pink + White' dissolves into birdsong and is replaced by the drumstick count-in and intoxicating Edge guitar riff of U2's 'One' and it casts a spell over the room and everything turns to liquid. So the wood of the desk no longer pushes up towards me, instead I push through it and come out as if through to the surface of water, and it becomes a portal to anywhere in time, I just need to let go and it'll take me. I land in a park near my old house. It was the park you taught me how to play football in.

We are on stage at Ward Park in Bangor, it is the summer of 2019. We are in the middle of playing 'What If This Storm Ends?'. If I tap my foot on a little button at my feet it cuts off my microphone to the audience and the sound instead goes directly to our monitor engineer Jamie at the side of the stage. That way if anything goes wrong during the gig I have a quick way of communicating with him. In this moment I am about to use that device to ask him a quick question.

The next song of the setlist is written down as 'One Night Is Not Enough', a song from our second album we haven't played in a long time. I feel a tiny bit bad for the song, it finally gets called up to the setlist after all this time and we have no intention of playing it. We will be playing a different song in its place as we have a secret special guest joining us to sing it. I click the foot pedal to talk to Jamie to find out if our guest has arrived. 'He's here,' came the two-word reply. My shoulders lower a bit with the news. You see, the gentleman that he is, he had done us a big favour but could only get here after we had taken to the stage already, so we wouldn't know he had definitely arrived until close to this song appearing on the setlist.

The final bars of 'What If This Storm Ends?' ebb away and we start playing the opening bars of this different song. As soon as I start singing it the crowd join in with gusto. 'Is it getting better? Or do you feel the same? Will it make it easier on you now? You got someone to blame.' The crowd and I sing the first verse and chorus like our lives depend on it. The second verse begins and out strolls Bono, just out for a walk in the park, which I guess he kinda was, and singing it with the swagger of the man that wrote it, which he definitely was. For all the gig stages he has ever stepped out onto all over the world it was the first time he had ever stepped onto one in Bangor, and Bangor let him know exactly how happy they were to see him on it. If there was a roof to the place they would have found it days later in the middle of the Irish Sea somewhere. It was a moment alright.

My dad had known for months that Ward Park was happening and would hear none of it when we said it might not be the right place for him. He really wasn't well by then but he was going to be there and that was that. 'If I'm alive I'm going,' he would say. By this stage though, his legs didn't work anymore so he would need to be in a wheelchair. He was also though now prone to saying the first thing that sprang to his mind with zero filter and we were pretty nervous anytime he was going anywhere near, y'know, humans because he would say something wildly inappropriate to someone. And the thought of him being around 35,000 someones was a bit nerve-racking for everyone in the family. Telling someone after they have just been insulted that the person that just levelled them has dementia may soften the blow a little but it's still hard for them to unhear. But anytime there was talk of him missing out there would be an argument, so talk switched to how, not if.

The whole family were out in the crowd in the VIP section but there was no way he could be out there of course, so two very kind people from the nursing home accompanied him to the backstage area. When he first arrives, and is finally in situ in his wheelchair looking around and taking it all in, sensing the moment he was party to, he takes my hand and delivers one of his catchphrases, 'You're some operator, son.' It was his way of saying he was proud of me. There's tears in his eyes. The two nursing staff wheel him up the steep ramp to the side of the stage just before the show started. In, at that time, 25 years of my parents coming to our gigs I don't think either of them had been side of stage at any show. They preferred to be out in the thick of it. I remember looking down at the Witness Festival (latterly called Oxygen, now defunct) once and, two songs into our set, I saw my mum in the front row, giving it socks with the best of them. It was a disconcerting sight I have to say, but looking back on it what an absolute legend she is. But here tonight I walk onto the stage past my father for the first time, and the last time. He would never see us play another show, as he would be gone six months from now.

Bono leaves the stage to rapture and we play the rest of a set that was one of the better nights we ever had on planet Earth. I get back to mine to find myself locked out of my house. Just in case you think any of this is glamorous and we all go to fancy parties with champagne and celebrities after shows like that. I sit on my doorstep for 45 minutes, ears ringing, heart still taking up all the real estate in my chest, all other organs in orbit around me until my heart allows them back in, much later.

The next day our wonderful assistant Natalie calls to tell me a story. Bono arrived side of stage about ten minutes before he was due to join us. He took up a spot nearby Natalie as it happened, and after about five minutes he pointed at the elderly gent in the wheelchair and asked her is that Gary's dad? She replied in the affirmative. He went straight over and chatted to my dad for the next five minutes and took pictures with him and was the kind legend he always is. This was the one and only time they met. He told my dad it was lovely to meet him, shook his hand one last time, and took a leisurely stroll out onto the stage to blow everyone's mind.

For the next six months until the day all the power of his speech finally deserted him, my dad would tell the story to anyone that would listen, about him and his great pal Bono, standing together (my dad was also standing in his version of the story) watching his son play at Ward Park to 40,000 people (yup, he would also bump up the number of people that were there too, it may have even got to 50k in some retellings). My mum, my sister, all my aunts, uncles and cousins were gutted not to meet Bono, and my dad would rub it in every chance he got. Jack got to hang out with Bono and they all missed out. As we say in Norn Iron: scundered for yis! So for the last part of his life my dad got to tell a story about him and his best mate Bono having the craic at Ward Park. It was his favourite story. And it's my favourite too.

Back through the aqueous desk portal that spits me out and slams me down on the solid-again table with a crack to the forehead. Fuck's sake! Or did I just drift off with my chin on my hands again trying to write something. I give up trying to write anything for the day and turn on the TV. There's a show I am on the last episode of I decide to finish. It's not light viewing but I'm determined to get to the end of it. I have been gravitating mostly to fluffy comedies and I am trying to push myself to watch some things a bit more substantial.

In the last few weeks I have felt something alter inside me a little. In my head, in my heart, in my atoms. But when I have tried to put my focus on it, it scurries away like an eye-floater. So, I'm not sure what it is exactly but it feels similar to that tonal shift on the banks of Strangford Lough from the fathomless night into a prelude of day. Black turning to the darkest deepest blue, barely noticeable, but turning all the same. An ice age coming to an end with the yearning release of the first cracking. The end of everything in this epoch, in this age. But can you really feel something new coming before it comes? Is there a hint of it? If you strip time and dates and numbers away from the universe do we make it easier or more difficult to know a change is coming? Do we need to be counted in, like some song we are about to sing? Or are there times when we just begin and we hit the first beat at exactly the right time, and we know it's perfect only because the moment itself tells us so? This edge I'm standing on, is it annihilation or a new world made from all the parts of the old? Minus one part of course. And will there be a hole shaped much like you in this possible world or will the blue that I paint this new landscape with leave no trace of you at all?

The TV show ends. Before the credits roll a Rumi quote appears on the screen one line at a time. I hadn't been aware of the quote before I don't think, though I went on to learn it was one of his more famous ones. Sometimes we miss these things, or they are deliberately kept from us so that they might be delivered at the exact right time. I had no idea that reading those words as they appeared on the screen would finally unfreeze the wound that was slashed into me a year ago, the wound that contained within it everything that had been deferred for so long, and I would feel it all at once, and it would be almost too much for me to feel.

And so the lines came one by one.

First ...

Out beyond ideas of wrongdoing and rightdoing

Then ...

There is a field

And finally ...

I will meet you there

Those words were sent that day to unlock me. They were a key. But I don't think they were the only key. In fact I am sure there were many sent to me by the universe over the last year and they just didn't land on me, or I didn't see them, or hear them, or the day they landed I just didn't want them.

But when these words take shape in front of me in a way that I understand, that key finally finds the lock and whatever door that was holding my grief at bay is opened, and behind it a torrent finally tumbles out. Not a single tear for 12 months and then suddenly they were rushing from me, like that dreamlike waterfall you fell into. They want me standing so I stand up, I place my hands on the back of my couch and lean forwards. I have never experienced anything like it and only know that it could happen at all because I was there, and it happened to me. Water pours out of my eyes. Not teardrops, not crying, pouring. Spilling. Everything that had been held, falls. The numbness falls away too. I feel pain for the first time in a long time. And I love that pain. When the tears stop falling I ball up on the couch and fall asleep.

I dream of you. We are fishing. That first time you took me. Off a pier somewhere in Ireland, no doubt not that far away from a caravan. No rods, we just have lines wrapped around wee wooden rectangles, wee weights on the lines a foot from a large hook and some bait I can't see in the dream. I feel safe because you are there. There is nothing that can hurt me because here's my da. My da's bigger than your da. Thing is, mine was. Bigger than all my mate's da's anyway. Here we are, me and my big da, fishing. With lines uncurled in the water from wee wooden rectangles. It could have been any point in the 200,000-year history of humanity, and just as I think that, in the background the buildings shrink away and horses and carts roll by, replaced with farmlands, then just trees as far as the eyes can see. A forest sprawls untamed. Us standing by both the edge of the water and the edge of the vast forest behind us, we the king and prince of everything before such words were even invented. Fallen beyond speech the two of us. Yet to be invented: speech, writing, history, the wheel, cars, planes, guns, caravans, television, anxiety, arguments, death. We will have to stay here and live without all those things. Just fishing for everything we need. Just me and my colossal father.

The next day I wake up and I feel it. Something is trying to get out. So I sit down. The pen feels different in my hand. Squat, snug as a gun. It wants to be there. And with it I write this song about you and call it 'The Long Shadow'. These are the words of it:

Bowled over like a hit and run
Don't go for goodness sake my son
Tears come for everyone but me
Oh why won't they come
I've none, what's fucking wrong with me
It's just cause you're numb
My friends tell me but my friends can't see
Inside of my head
I'm broken every word spoken
Well they just make me mad
I don't wanna cry and I don't wanna watch these people
  cry
I don't wanna know and I don't wanna open up my eyes
I want you not to die
I want you not to die
Time freezes when your light retracts
No Jesus but I'm told he'll be back
Sing softly so the house won't fall
Can you hear the phone
I think roughly 'bout a thousand calls
Oh just leave me alone
Time passes but the numbness lasted
And now I'm here in your coat
Raising glasses to you in some past mist
It feels like blood in my throat
I don't want to hope and I don't want to hear it cools with
  time

I don't want to speak and maybe I don't want it to be fine
I want you not to die
I want you not to die

It flowed from the pen in one fluid motion. It took five minutes to write. Sometimes songs do. Sometimes they take five years ('Life on Earth', I'm talking to you) but sometimes, if you're very lucky, they take five or ten or thirty minutes. I paint some very simple chords onto it and it hangs together very nicely. We would play some acoustic tours in the next few years and this song would become a regular feature of those tours. We'd also try to record a version of it for this album but we just never got it quite right. Not sure why. Sometimes you just get the sense that a song may not find the right shape, or sound, or time. Maybe its time will come. Maybe not.

Later that day though, I write another song. This one is definitely not about you. It is about all the regret I feel about something else entirely. I wrote a song on the last album called 'What If This Is All the Love You Ever Get'. I thought while I was writing it that it was about a friend of mine who was going through a tough time. Turns out it was about me. That happens sometimes. Songs are funny that way, they'll only tell you what they're about when they think you can handle the truth of it. But, conversely, sometimes you know immediately, and as I put pen to paper on this same day about all the hurt I have caused, the words start to bleed out and I know right away this is my regret, and not someone else's …

I'm not gonna lie to you anymore
After these lies then no more …

The rest of the song follows behind those first two lines almost as quickly as 'The Long Shadow' did. This song, 'These Lies', would turn out to be the first one written for *The Forest Is the Path*. Two songs, after no songs for a year, that seem to ride out on a river of energy dammed inside for a long time. Is it then the ice of you melting in me that sent these songs through my pen and out onto the page? I had worried a year before that I would never hear from you again, that I would never get to ask you anything again, that I would not know where you are and if you were anywhere at all. Turns out you were holding up the scaffolding of my whole world so it wouldn't fall until I could hold it all by itself. So you were Atlas tasked not with holding up the entire universe, but instead holding up the fabric of just one person's existence. Until I let go, you couldn't let go either. The world is only heavy if you try to lift it. When I put it down, I understand, this was always when I was supposed to put it down.

I don't know if you're at peace now that you're not holding up the whole goddamn world for me but I do hope you are. I don't know if the hole in the world you left behind will ever fill in completely but I hope that it doesn't. I don't know what the atoms you left behind will turn into, but I know they will build new life and that life will endure. I don't know if I'll ever forgive myself for the things I said to you but I am sorry, and even though I know I can never tell you in your lifetime, I can tell you in mine, so let me say that I am sorry dad, for it all, for everything I put you through, and I hope that these words find you wherever you are. And finally, I really and truly don't know much of anything at all, but one of the few things I do know is that in this life and all past and future lives happening all at once and never and always, you are my father and I love you.